ASSOCIATION FOR COMPUTER AIDED DESIGN IN ARCHITECTURE
LIFE in:formation
ON RESPONSIVE INFORMATION AND VARIATIONS IN ARCHITECTURE

Title: LIFE in:formation
                On Responsive Information and Variations in Architecture

                Exhibition Catalog of the 30th Annual Conference of Association for Computer Aided Design in Architecture, ACADIA

Editors: Chandler Ahrens, Axel Schmitzberger, Michael Wen-Sen Su

Conference Chairs: Aaron Sprecher , McGill University, Montreal
                        Shai Yeshayahu, Southern Illinois University
                        Pablo Lorenzo-Eiroa, The Cooper Union, New York

Exhibition Chairs: Chandler Ahrens, Founding Partner Open Source Architects
                        Axel Schmitzberger, California State Polytechnic University, Pomona
                        Michael Wen-Sen Su, The Pratt Institute

Design Coordinator: Axel Schmitzberger

Copy Editor: Quynh T. Nguyen,

Graphic Design: Axel Schmitzberger, Tony Martínez, Ice Lee (starfish-prime.com)

Typeface: Pill Gothic, Rotis Sans Serif, Netto, Helvetica, News Gothic

Printing: Printinghouse, Inc., WI

Websites: www.acadia.org/acadia2010

                        Library of Congress Control Number: 2010934914
                        Life in:formation, On Responsive Information and Variations in Architecture, Exhibition Catalog
                        eds. Chandler Ahrens, Axel Schmitzberger and Micahel Wen-Sen Su, New York 2010.
                        174 pages, 8.5x11in
                        Printed in the United States of America.
                        ISBN 978-1-4507-3472-1

Peer Reviewing Committte for ACADIA 2010 - LIFE in:formation

Sherif Abdelmohsen
PhD Candidate, Georgia
Institute of Technology

Emily Abruzzo
Assistant Professor,
Parson School of Art

Henri Achten
Associate Professor, Czech
Technical University in Prague

Chandler Ahrens
Founding Partner,
Open Source Architecture

Phillip Anzalone
Director, Building Technology
Sequence, Columbia University

Phillip Beesley
Associate Professor,
University of Waterloo

Torben Berns
Visiting Professor,
McGill University

Oliver Bertram
Assistant Professor University
of Applied Art, Vienna

Gail Borden
Assistant Professor, USC

Meredith Bostwick
Senior Associate
Architect, RMJM

Martin Bressani
Associate Professor,
McGill University

Anthony Caicco
Visiting Lecturer,
The Ohio State University,
Knowlton School of Architecture

Guedi Capeluto
Senior Lecturer,
Technion - Israel Institute
of Technology

Sheng-Fen Chien
Assistant Professor,
National Cheng Kung University

Jason Crow
PhD Candidate,
McGill University

Christian Derix
Head of Computational Design
and Research, AEDAS

Edouard Din
Associate Professor
of Architecture,
Tuskegee University

Marty Doscher
Director of Information
Technology,
Morphosis Architects

Jose Pinto Duarte
Assistant Professor,
TU Lisbon

Jeremy Ficca
Assistant Professor,
Carnegie Mellon University

Pia Fricker
Chair for CAAD,
ETH, Zurich

Paola Giaconia
Professor of Architectural
Design, California State
University in Florence

Michael D. Gibson
Instructor / Researcher,
Ball State University

Marcelyn Gow
Design Faculty, Royal Institute
of Technology, Stockholm

Yasha Grobman
PhD, Technion - Israel Institute
of Technology

Mark D. Gross
Professor, Carnegie Mellon
University

Gilles Halin
Research Director, MAP-CRAI
Laboratory, Nancy University

Michael Hensel
Professor, AHO Oslo

Christiane M. Herr
Visiting Assistant Professor,
National Cheng Kung University

Alicia Imperiale
Assistant Professor,
Temple University

Mehlika Inanici
Assistant Professor,
University of Washington

Jason Johnson
Assistant Professor,
Calgary University

Omar Khan
Associate Professor,
University of Buffalo

Joachim B. Kieferle
Professor,
Hochschule RheinMain

Axel Kilian
Assistant Professor,
Princeton University

Yoshihiro Kobayashi
Research Associate,
Arizona State University

Branko Kolarevic
Professor, Calgary University

Robert J. Krawczyk
Associate Professor,
Illinois Institute of Technology

Peter Lang
Associate Professor,
Texas A&M University

Tapani Launis
PhD, Architecture Tapani Launis

Brian Lilley
Associate Professor,
Dalhousie University

Mark Linder
Professor, Syracuse University

Brian Lockyear
Principal, Lockyear Design

Pablo Lorenzo-Eiroa
Associate Professor,
Adjunct The Cooper Union

Gregory A. Luhan
Associate Professor
of Architecture,
University of Kentucky

Alexis Meier
Associate Professor,
National Institute of Applied
Sciences, Strasbourg

Miguel Mesa del Castillo
Technical Specialist,
Politécnica Superior
de Architectura del Alicante

Rafael Gomez Moriana
Adjunct Associate Professor,
University of Calgary

Hoda Moustapha
PhD Computational Design,
Carnegie Mellon University

Eduardo S. Nardelli
Professor Adjunto, Universidade
Presbiteriana Mackenzie

Eran Neuman
Chair, School of Architecture
Tel Aviv University

Yeonjoo Oh
PhD Candidate, CoDeLab,
Carnegie Mellon University

Filiz Ozel
Professor of Architecture
and Landscape Architecture,
Arizona State University

Murali Paranandi
Associate Professor
of Architecture,
Miami University

Vera Parlac
Assistant Professor,
Calgary University

Atilio Pentimalli
Instructor,
University of Buenos Aires

Santiago R. Perez
Assistant Professor
of Architecture,
University of Arkansas

Christopher Pierce
Unit Master, AA

Celine Pinet
Dean of Instruction,
West Valley College

Alessandra Ponte
Associate Professor,
Université de Montréal

George Proctor
Professor, California
State Polytechnic
University, Pomona

David Ruy
Assistant Professor,
The Pratt Institute

Jenny Sabin
Lecturer, University
of Pennsylvania

Antonino Saggio
Professor, Universita
La Sapienza, Rome

Andrew Saunders
Assistant Professor,
Rensselaer
Polytechnic Institute

Axel Schmitzberger
Associate Professor,
California State Polytechnic
University, Pomona

Marc Aurel Schnabel
Associate Professor,
The Chinese University
of Hong Kong

Mohamed Sharif
Associate Professor,
OTIS College of Art and Design

Mark Shepard
Assistant Professor,
University of Buffalo

Pedro Soza
Assistant Professor,
Univesidad de Chile

Ryan E. Smith
Assistant Professor,
University of Utah

Aaron Sprecher
Assistant Professor,
McGill University

Joshua Stein
Associate Professor,
Woodbury University

Marc Swackhamer
Assistant Professor,
University of Minnesota

Michael Wen-Sen Su
Visiting Professor,
The Pratt Institute

Kyle Talbott
Associate Professor,
University of
Wisconsin-Milwaukee

Joshua Taron
Assistant Professor,
Calgary University

Aron Temkin
Dean, Norwich University

Oliver Tessmann
Bollinger + Grohmann Ingenieure

Lisa Tilder
Associate Professor,
The Ohio State University,
Knowlton School of Architecture

David Theodore
PhD Candidate,
Harvard University

Graziano Mario Valenti
Professor, R.A.D.A.A.R.
Universita La Sapienza, Rome

Eric Verboon
Façade Designer,
Buro Happold

Shane Williamson
Associate Professor,
University of Toronto

Wei Yan
Assistant Professor,
Texas A&M University

Shai Yeshayahu
Associate Professor,
Southern Illinois University

So-Yeon Yoon
Assistant Professor,
University of Missouri-Columbia

Table of Contents

Introductions

author: **Nancy Yen-wen Cheng**

organization: President, ACADIA

country: United States

Digital Seeds

The ACADIA 2010 designers are exploring how digital technology can create meaningful forms, intense experiences, and better performance. They are defining an aesthetic sensibility inspired by nature and processed through algorithms, circuitry, and assemblies. Whereas yesterday's machines strived for a reliable uniformity, today's digital devices mimic natural mechanisms and heighten awareness of nature. Responsive surfaces accentuate ambient physical forces and our physiological reactions. For example, the Fibre Composite Adaptive System dynamically adapts a flexible tessellation to temperature and humidity changes through neural networks. Related work brings together the planned and the serendipitous so that geometric forms can dance with light and participants (i.e., Vox flowbody, Xeromax sensing envelope, and Morpholuminescence).

To follow the Life in Formation metaphor, each project is a seedling of a new idea whose germination is supported by a bundle of stored energy. A seedling's energy is directed to the growing tips of the shoots and roots, where undifferentiated cells adapt into the anticipated plant structure. In a similar way, a project's energy is expended at the unknown frontier, transforming according to requirements of its context. A plant whose shoots are cut redirects its growing energy to emerge in a new area, and a designer facing an impediment uses lateral thinking to find new solutions.

The increasing legacy of digital solutions provides a foundation for artist-designers through aesthetic inspirations and technical models. But the same crowdsource that provides robust tech support also bombards us with motion and noise, and makes today's innovation quickly grow stale. So to create a project these days takes a leap of faith. It takes an optimistic attitude that despite the over-saturation of digital marketing, there could be a moment of repose where the quality of a space or the subtlety of a detail could make a difference.

Designers are searching to find meaning in this parametric world of endless variation. For example, the HWYLtL project translates survey data into sublime drawings that we can't rationally parse. Nanotechnica's structures brings us on a fantastic voyage into the world of an electron microscope. Both projects invite us to read the hieroglyphics of a new language. The question emerges, would analyzing our intuitive perceptions enhance or kill this unexpected beauty?

These forward-looking projects conceptually position themselves to transform architectural practice, whether through literally knitting new composite materials or metaphorically knitting together a landscape. Through the Listener membrane, the author* shows how textile manufacturing techniques can generate custom "information-based materials" and invites us to create new rapid prototyping options for architecture. At the other end of the scale, the Detroit Superdivision project shows how to revive a wasted urban fabric by colonizing and re-contextualizing the familiar with a few big moves.

Especially in an economic recession, the designers seek maximal effect though minimal means: What thoughtful steps and processes can make a difference? Digital projects may start with a hammer looking for the right nail, with small experimental vehicles showing the potential of the media. Designers are using art installations to discover how spatial proximity, surface movement, and dynamic lighting can enhance experience. Experimenting with decorative surfaces and connection details can stimulate ideas about material manipulations, tectonic relationships, and viewer perceptions that can grow beyond the room scale. In viewing these projects, we need to remember that even small seeds can grow quickly. By planting them in our imagination, we can fertilize new territories, to let their promise inform visions of new buildings, cities, and landscapes.

author: **Michael Wen-Sen Su**

organization: Pratt Institute, School of Architecture

country: United States

Change Your Head
in:Formation on Exhibition Selection

Considering both his extensive involvement with the Independent Group and his recent experiences in America, the choice of artist John McHale as guest editor for the "Marginalia" section of the May, 1957 issue of *The Architectural Review* was not altogether surprising. As well, while McHale's decision to focus on the latest and strangest of American technology may have been somewhat unusual, previous "Marginalia" have featured, through blog-like briefs, a veritable cornucopia of the interesting and odd. Besides, as its subtitle "Machine Made, America II" indicated, this issue was a special number dedicated to the coverage of recent achievements of America's emergent industrial, architectural might. That is, it continued the coverage of an earlier, 1950 issue on "Man Made, America." Rather, what truly distinguished this particular issue was McHale's contribution to its cover: an extraordinary collage assembled from bright, colorful fragments of freshly-imported Americana to depict a misshapen, but clearly identifiable, head.

According to executive editor Ian McCallum, whereas the Review's earlier investigation registered a "record of sprawl and visual squalor...the record of a failure," the sequel found a "success story—the story of how America is adding sheer quantity to the pre-existing qualities of modern architecture." For McHale, specifically, editing Marginalia afforded him the opportunity to curate selections from his now-famous steamer-trunk, which he had filled during his recent visit to America with the latest in machine-made, i.e. pamphlets and journals printed with vibrant colors on machines not yet available in England. Still, the progression from man- to machine-made, from quality to quantity, and from failure to success hardly seemed able to account for the incongruous cover—particularly for an architectural journal. McHale's collage was especially striking for its unmistakable likeness to "Robby the Robot," the surprisingly-witty, immediately-iconic robot from the previous year's MGM film *The Forbidden Planet*. Rather than merely mimicking Robby's famously bulbous head, however, McHale's variant was decidedly more unsettling: besides being constructed from bushings, sparkplugs, and pistons, it was also built with pieces of chocolate cake, "infrared-cooked" steak, and canned ham. The resulting composite was easily more appropriate for the cover of some transgressive, even-more fantastical magazine conjoining the mechanically-inclined *Astounding Science Fiction* and biologically-oriented *Galaxy Science Fiction*. Nonetheless, this was precisely the juxtaposition McHale sought to evoke, for he found Robby's clean-cut, purely-mechanical composition—and, by extension, screenwriter Cyril Hume's update of Issac Asimov's 1940 "Robbie"—to be seriously deficient. Instead, and even beyond the context of speculating upon the future of merely "machine made" architecture for The Architectural Review, McHale's collage dramatically depicted the inevitable convergence of man and machine, and thereby asserted the impossibility for architecture to remain aloof or unchanged by the rising tide of scientific and technological progress. If European architecture might have been characterized as more machine-like, or more formal, while developing American architecture was perceived as more machine-made, or performative, then McHale's wayward collage actually speculated upon a future of architecture, which fused the formal and performative into what may be termed the purely machinic. Driven neither solely by formal considerations, or that of "hardware", nor performative requirements, or that of "software", McHale's vision of the machinic blended the mechanical and organic to produce a variable, dynamic architecture—and, by extension, its underlying design strategies and processes—incorporating aspects of both hardware and software. Indeed, he virtually declared as much two years earlier in an article decrying the unfulfilled promises of Walter Gropius and his Bauhaus: "Previously it was possible to think in terms of eternal basic conditions, now we have to learn to think in terms of a self-changing basis." [Emphasis added.] In other words, McHale's Marginalia and his extraordinary collage may well be construed as a precedent for the present ACADIA 2010 exhibition titled "Evolutive Means: On Adaptation and Selection in Architectural Design."

As its title suggests, the present exhibition invokes the notions of adaptation and selection to characterize certain design strategies in architecture. Most generally, these are inter-disciplinary, multi-valence design strategies, which explicitly treat architecture as a parametric-testing environment by initiating collaborations between architects and, for instance, artists and engineers, to organize and render, or distill, into legible information the otherwise infinite and impenetrable data comprising our built environment. Architecture itself, from this particular perspective, operates as a computing environment consisting of both software and hardware, or programs and platforms, ranging from boundary conditions to physical site, from analysis software to milling machines, or most simply, from idea to "final" product. However, this process of distillation is non-linear, as the intrinsic variability of both data and data-processing entails the continuous "feedback" of any resulting information to its originating strategies for "optimization" of both the structures of the collaboration and the actual processing of data. This manner of feedback and optimization infers the non-linear adaptation and selection, or self-changing, "evolutive" regulation, of the design strategy. That is, in addition to the mere feedback and optimization of parameters passed to procedures, evolutive design strategies modulate, or oscillate, procedures towards optimal performance of the entire system by construing outcomes as more or less usable, legible, or most simply, "fit", with respect to the initiating parameters, designated procedures, and requisite performances. Thus, more than merely computer-aided, and neither solely machine-like nor machine-made, these strategies are intrinsically machinic. As a result, and commensurate with the pervasive deployment of exponentially more capable computation throughout architecture, the projects they have produced and the design territory they have circumscribed have, of late, been especially resistant to assessment, whether generally, or through either purely formal or strictly performative measures.

"Evolutive Means: On Adaptation and Selection in Architectural Design" explores this challenging design territory with the exhibition of the narrative histories of 15 peer-reviewed projects displayed at The Great Hall Gallery of The Cooper Union and 12 curated projects presented in the Siegel Gallery of The Pratt Institute. These projects have distinguished themselves, either through explicit invitation or blind peer-review, by the generative, iterative, or otherwise self-changing, evolutive design strategies underlying the four stages of their development: conceptualization, design, fabrication, and ultimately, utilization. Crucially, while these strategies may be characterized as machinic, the implied convergence of the formal and performative, or of hardware and software, is neither uniform nor equal across all four stages of these projects. Rather, the balances may shift, back-and-forth, between the formal and performative, and from stage to stage. For instance, whereas projects such as *Voxel, Morpholuminescence, Listener,* and *Behavior, not Intelligence* may seem purely performative in utilization, or software driven, especially with respect to the interactivity of the environments they attempt to generate, their conceptualization and design were still motivated by formal, albeit iterative, considerations. Conversely, if the structural software and performance testing of projects like *Lux Nova, Aortic Arc, 0-14,* and the *Fiber*

Composite Adaptive System may have dominated their design and fabrication stages, the realized project is certainly "utilized" more formally, or as hardware. At the same time, other projects like H*eterogeneity, Nanotectonica, Klex,* and *Latent Figure Protocol* perch delicately on the fine line between the formal and performative throughout their development. Irrespective of the distributions of their formal or performative balances, all 27 projects consistently demonstrate the overall, non-linear adaptation and selection, or self-changing "evolutive" regulation, of their underlying design strategies. As such, they cannot be characterized merely as the convergence between the formal and performative. Rather, as both the presentation of the narrative histories of these projects and the contextualization of these histories within the thematic matrix of the ACADIA 2010 Conference demonstrate, this machinic bifurcation may be integrated fluidly, iteratively, and never definitively.

Besides his extraordinary cover for *The Architectural Review*, McHale ventured to offer one further speculation upon the future of man and machine, of the machinic. In his "Marginalia", he also included a rather peculiar picture of himself holding up a bundle of magazine scraps, bits of metal and machinery, and rolled-up string, which together formed a misshapen, only-vaguely identifiable head. Perhaps by way of advocating for the eventuality of embracing the emergent "self changing basis" of architecture, and certainly in reference to his alternative version of Robby the Robot, McHale captioned this photograph: "John McHale, with his 'spare head'."

author: **Axel Schmitzberger**
organization: California State Polytechnic University, Pomona

country: United States

We are the Robots
Intelligent Patterns - Authoring Information

We love redundancy. We like the idea that things—though minutely different—are generally re-occurring. There is comfort in reoccurring structures and patterns. We like to extract portions of content and reassure ourselves that this information only contains a partial variation or differentiation to previously collected and stored information; if information would be all new, systems would collapse. We would collapse.

Information is easier to measure than to describe; while it is easy to measure the quantity based on agreed standards, quality can be assessed by projecting meaning or layered representative value to elements *(Lloyd, 2006)*. Its etymological roots suggest to give shape and meaning to something, hence the intrinsic relationship to broadly disseminated terms μορφή *(morphe)* "form" and also εἶδος *(eidos)* "kind, idea, shape, set". Admitting to these interdependencies, it is necessary to instantly acknowledge and address repetition and difference and respectively aspects of semblance such as representation and manifestation *(Deleuze,1968)*. This in turn raises the question about the relevance of giving shape to things through meaning, which indicates that the problem of authorship is connected to the issue of redundancy, originality, and feedback scenarios.

However, looking beyond the final chapters of the Information Age and being fully immersed in the early years of the Nano-Neuroage, attention currently turns away from traditional methods of forming and shaping towards operating self-propellant systems that seem to question the principle of authorship. Feedback scenarios inherently submit to an ideomotor effect once they are considered intelligent. These days we create an understanding that even cloud formations are reoccurring patterns subordinated to rules of complex algorithms; however, we insist on the importance of curatorial decisions, authoring content as it is submitted into matrices that are used to form partial re-creations of otherwise natural systems. This seemingly paradoxical condition is part of a larger relevant oscillating, cybernetic organization (we may as well call it organism). Such micrology of unstableness can be visualized by the diagrammatic representaion of Spencer Brown's *tetralemma* *(Baecker, 2002) (Figure 1)*.

Through communication itself we are able to differentiate within a system; we are establishing an asymmetrical relationship to an environment within which the system exists *(among other systems)*. The form and grade of differentiation allows us to determine the intelligence of the system which however can be only defined by an outside world that cannot be defined without defining new environments and systems. The fifth position is taken by the weak re-entry or implicit context - the field in which the system communicates with itself about its environment and the strong re-entry in which the system reflects within the environment about its decision.

Figure 1. Graphic interpretation of Spencer Brown's Tetralemma (S = system, E = environment)

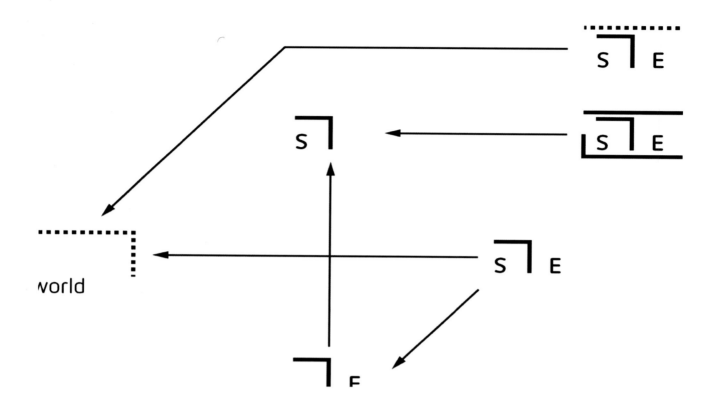

Three images of the International Space Station *(ISS)* serve as example of such interaction of systems. Figure 2 shows the ISS viewed from earth with a far-range telescope camera; figure 3 shows the same object viewed from a 195 km distance taken by a German satellite using radar-visualization technology; figure 4 shows an image taken from a space shuttle undocking the space station (Figure 2, 3, & 4). All three images reveal different information, spatially, temporally, quantitatively, and qualitatively. All three images are taken from within discreet systems, however those systems communicate with each other as they are describing the same object. We can now synthesize the three different information heaps through a feedback procedure and increase the quantitative and also qualitative representational value.

Figure 2. International Space Station, captured on the 25/09/2008.

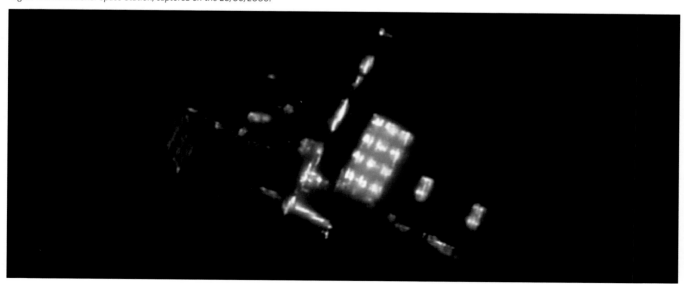

Figure 3. Radar image of the International Space (ISS) by TerraSAR-X

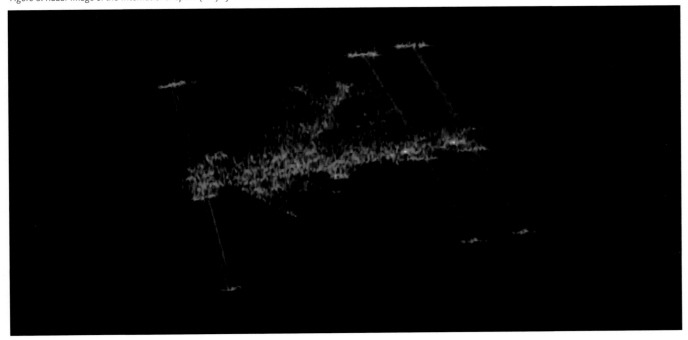

Figure 4. Shuttle Mission S126-E-014792 (28 Nov. 2008) Undocking of the shuttle from the ISS

Communication is key to developing meaning *(Lloyd, 2006)*. Information is valueless if it cannot enter a system with which it can interact or is adopted by a system which assigns value to the egalitarian, neutral data-stream. Communication requires common parameters, patterns— recognizable features—to enable differentiation and thus engage intelligence. Correspondingly, the General Inter-Action Scheme *(G.I.A.S.)*, which is presented as a graphic interpretation of an Uexkuell based human behavioral mapping model, was developed in the late 1970s to understand interaction of elements in the area of human ecology *(Knoetig, 1980)*. The model reveals a distinct relationship and principle to the tetralemma, enabling differentiation via feedback scenarios *(Figure 5)*.

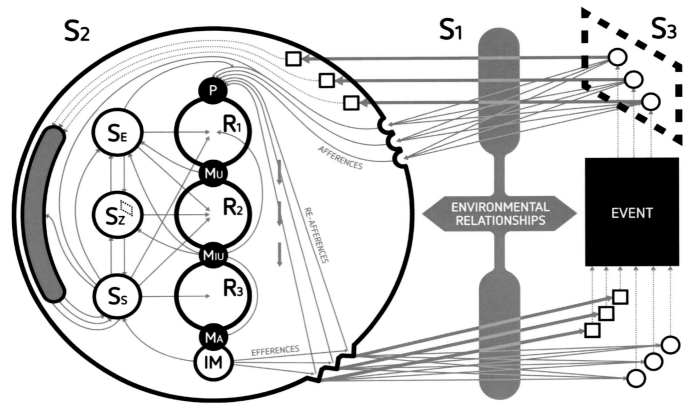

Figure 5. G.I.A.S. (homo sapiens)
Complex, complete visualization of the G.I.A.S. (homo sapiens) and the different relationships between the three systems in repect to S2 (human) and its processes and calculations. („S1": Environmental Relationships, „S2": Homo Sapiens, „S3": enviornment; „P": ppresentation of S3 factos; S"E": memory experience; S"Z": ,memeory goals; S"S": Speicher Status; M"U": Model of the environment; M"IU": model of human in its environment; M"A": model of activities; R1-3: calculationsteps 1-3; „IM": Impulsmatrix)

Now, after the peak of the development in *generative- or emergent-design-ism*, we once again allow the observation of recurrence; this enables us to standardize input-output, feedback, and, respectively, a sensory apparatus that develops meaning (influence) based upon opulent data (affluence), thus synergizing confluence. Our agency, however, is limited by the structure—the recurrent arrangements that seem to influence and limit our choices. Demanding discreet authenticity develops isolation, therefore it is hermetic and somewhat architecturally autistic. In a traditional sense, an architectural proposal inherently desires originality; in critical terms, it can be understood as having an identity with itself, which—as Adorno suggests—is an identity that in empirical reality is violently forced on all objects as identity with the subject and thus travestied. For him an aesthetic identity seeks to aid the non-identical *(Adorno, 1997)*. In his words, "the artwork is at once process and instant"*(Adorno, 1997)*. The amorphous condition without objectification or objectivity allows a true artwork. In this sense, we don't require authorship in its individualistic form, but we need to have an understanding of an operand and operation only. It is systematic.

Acadia 2010—life:in:formation purposefully looks into recurrence, resemblance, redundancy, and patterns; we observe and examine repeated conditions which have been crowd-sourced, data-mined, and revolved into another system to test their adaptability and, respectively, examine potential intelligent behavior. We want to witness and inspect all circumstances that are either unique or repetitive. In Acadia 2010—life:in:formation, we reach out to overcome the crisis of semblance by attempting to utilize a pool of data, crafting a whole that is substantial, rather than a series of differentiated, partial elements *(Adorno, 1997)*. Individual authorship is not dismissed but subordinated to an authoring of procedural events, eventually redefining the term authorship as a curatorial, nodal technique, infusing and controlling the self-generating systems. Thus we are looking beyond the attempt to create.

Architecture is, in itself, affluent, hence it is not the morphology that is of interest but, instead, what is in control of such and how intelligent it e- or involves. It is paramount for Architecture to finally mature and step outside the -isms. Therefore we put ourselves to work here: we are subservient to the operation by instilling planned subroutines. We over and over again (ad nauseum) ask for input and refine the filtering mechanisms through feedback in order to sustain intelligence.

What remains is the issue of self-reference/closure when the operand is identical to the operator *(Baecker, 2005)*; but when the Self is viewed as an operation used upon itself, then the span of duration may be the condition that resolves self-referential issues temporally and, respectively, spatially.

And it is time: "we are charging our batteries and now we are full of energy" *(Kraftwerk, 1978)*.

Imagecredits:

Figure 1: Brown's Tatralemma, graphic based on Baecker, D., Wozu Systeme? (transl.: Why Systems?) (2002), source: axel schmitzberger

Figure 2: International Space Station, captured on the 25/09/2008, Photo by Ralf Vandebergh. Found at HYPERLINK "http://www.mikesalway.com.au/blog/2009/07/17/amazing-images-of-the-international-space-station/" http://www.mikesalway.com.au/blog/2009/07/17/amazing-images-of-the-international-space-station/

Figure 3: Snapshot of the International Space. On March 13, 2008, the International Space Station passed across the field-of-view of Germany's remote sensing satellite, TerraSAR-X, at a distance of 195 kilometers, or 122 miles, and at a relative speed of 34,540 kilometers per hour, or more than 22,000 mph. The radar image of the station looks like a dense collection of bright spots from which the outlines of the space station can be clearly identified. The central element on the station, to which all the modules are docked, has a grid structure that presents a multiplicity of reflecting surfaces to the radar beam, making it readily identifiable. This image has a resolution of about one meter (about 39 inches). In other words, objects can be depicted as discrete units--that is, shown separately--provided that they are at least one meter apart. If they are closer together than that, they tend to merge into a single block on a radar image. Image Credit: DLR found at

Figure 4: S126-E-014792 (28 Nov. 2008) --- Backdropped by a blue and white Earth and the blackness of space, the International Space Station is seen from Space Shuttle Endeavour as the two spacecraft begin their relative separation. Earlier the STS-126 and Expedition 18 crews concluded 11 days, 16 hours and 46 minutes of cooperative work onboard the shuttle and station. Undocking of the two spacecraft occurred at 8:47 a.m. (CST) on Nov. 28, 2008. Found at HYPERLINK "http://spaceflight.nasa.gov/gallery/images/shuttle/sts-126/lores/s126e014918.jpg" http://spaceflight.nasa.gov/gallery/images/shuttle/sts-126/html/s126e014792.html

Figure 5: G.I.A.S. (homo sapiens) Complex, complete visualization of the G.I.A.S. (homo sapiens) and the different relationships between the three systems in repect to S2 (human) and its processes and calculations. („S1": Environmental Relationships, „S2": Homo Sapiens, „S3": enviornment; „P": ppresentation of S3 factos; S"E": memory experience; S"Z": ,memeory goals; S"S": Speicher Status; M"U": Model of the environment; M"IU": model of human in its environment; M"A": model of activities; R1-3: calculationsteps 1-3; „IM": Impulsmatrix) Source: Knoetig, H. (1980), folia oecologiae hominis, Humanoekologische Blaetter 9 ,45-130

Endnotes

Adorno, T. (1997). Aesthetische Theorie [English], In Aesthetic Theory, eds. G. Adorno and R. Tiedermann, 4-5, Minneapolis: University of Minnesota Press.

Baecker, D. (2002), Wozu Systeme?, 10-76, Berlin: Kulturverlag Kadmos

Deleuze, G. (1968), Difference et repetition [English, 1994 transl. Patton, P.], 104, New York: Columbia University Press
The whole theory of repetition is [...] subordinated to the requirements of simple representation, from the standpoint of its realism, materialism and subjectivism. Repetition is subjected to a principle of identity in the former present and a rule of resemblance in the present one.

Knoetig, H. (1980), folia oecologiae hominis, Humanoekologische Blaetter 9 ,45-130, Vienna: TU Wien

Kraftwerk, (1978), The Robots, Songlyrics., Duesseldorf: Kling Klang Music

Lloyd, S. (2006), Programming the Universe, a quantum computer scientist takes on the cosmos, 24-27, New York: Alfred A. Knopf

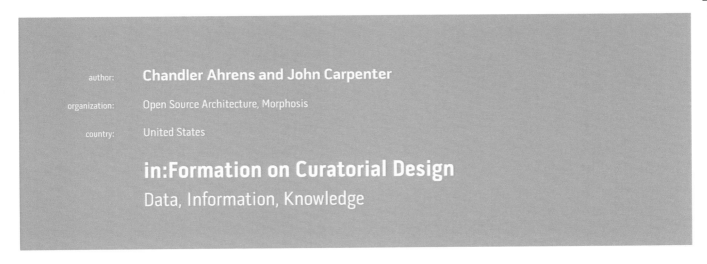

author: **Chandler Ahrens and John Carpenter**

organization: Open Source Architecture, Morphosis

country: United States

in:Formation on Curatorial Design
Data, Information, Knowledge

On December 5th, 2009, the Defense Advanced Research Projects Agency announced the DARPA Network Challenge to mark the 40th anniversary of the Internet. The challenge, open to any individual or team, consisted of being the first to submit the locations of 10 moored, 8-foot, red, weather balloons at 10 fixed locations in the continental United States. The geolocational challenge promoted the development of a social network strategy amongst a wide-area community for collecting, mining, and organizing large amounts of data. In addition to the large quantity of data was the issue of time in terms of both the speed of analyzing data flows and being to find the most current information. In the end, the MIT Red Balloon team won taking less than 9 hours to find all 10 locations.

DARPA's intent behind holding the competition was to learn how different teams created processes to solve the problem. In the end, the team with the most effective tool in terms of speed, quantity, and reliability of parsing data flows won the challenge. The role of developing computationally based tools to assist in a time-critical procedure for combing through large quantities of data to find useful information has significant resonance to a wide range of technologically based fields. The development of similar computational tools increasingly influences technologically oriented design professions and in particular those within the ACADIA community.

As computationally focused design professions begin to integrate information technologies into their design processes, new opportunities to analyze and parse the data for utilization in a generative design process are beginning to emerge. The nature of the information as well as the means to gather, organize, and filter data has a significant impact on the ability to determine its relevance and ultimately its usefulness. The speed at which data is generated and mined in the last few decades has increased exponentially as researchers, designers and "scientists collect more data than we as humans can perceive," promoting the importance of being able to understand the flow of information and not just specific components. Large quantities of data contain latent potential to be analyzed and transformed into information where it can be utilized in the design process, resulting in knowledge. The constant flow of ever-increasing amounts of data requires a real-time method for parsing the data to determine relevance to a specific discourse. While search engines such as Google News routes information generated from other sources into a single interface, relying on other sources to transform data into information without providing insight into the relevance of that information. In contrast, developing a method to traverse the tri-phase transition from data to information to knowledge provides a consistent procedure to ensure relevance within a particular discourse.

Data, as the most reduced level of abstraction from which information and knowledge originates, needs to be parsed in order to discover relevant patterns. Data-mining is a process to uncover quantitative or qualitative patterns from a larger database. Relevance of that data is determined by the method of filtration; therefore, the design of the computationally based data-mining process is highly subjective in order to transform the relevant data into useful information.

Information derived from a larger database inherently discloses, quantitatively or qualitatively, ideas generated by the community that formed the data. Similar to the process utilized in the DARPA Network Challenge, it is becoming increasingly common to implement Crowdsourcing to parse relevant information and the ideas that derive the information. While typically utilized for outsourcing problem solving to a large network of people, as in the DARPA challenge, the opportunity of utilizing Crowdsourcing is that the process of exploring a specific issue or discourse by many people generates multiple patterns and flows of ideas. In that sense, Crowdsourcing is a collaborative process that explores ideas that are relevant to a specific networked community at a specific time. In other words, relative to the speed of change in technologically oriented communities, it is more than a survey of what is happening now. It uncovers patterns of ideas that discuss orders of magnitude and relevance to that community.

Locating patterns of information provides the opportunity to establish relationships between ideas and to form knowledge about those ideas relative to a larger discourse. With the goal of developing relationships as a key focus of the curatorial design of the ACADIA exhibition, creating a tool that facilitates the transition from data to information to knowledge allows the curator to manage the flows of information. This work does not aim to replace the curator, but instead provides an opportunity to generate a critique or commentary of specific ideas relative to a larger discourse.

Design Process
The main focus of the ACADIA 2010 exhibition design process is to uncover patterns of information that can be used to generate knowledge about contemporary technological issues in the ACADIA community. Given that the conference is an annual event, the discourse within the ACADIA community constantly shifts and evolves. Thus, one of the first goals relies on the assembly of a current body of work from the ACADIA community to create a database. The next step involves mining the database to uncover quantitative pattern formations. Analysis of those formations uncover relationships that generate key concepts that describe the discourse upon which individual projects in the exhibition can be compared. Establishing relationships from the quantitative and qualitative attributes informs the computational algorithm that generates a self-organizing exhibition design. This process allows new patterns between the selected projects to emerge while maintaining relativity to the larger ACADIA community and generating knowledge of the current discourse *(Figure 1).*

Assembling a current body of work from the ACADIA community to form the database coincided with the submission of projects and papers for the 2010 conference. Aggregating all the texts provides a database that contains a wide range of current ideas from scent generating space to responsive fabrics being investigated within the community. The submission process for all papers and projects involves uploading to OpenConf, which is a management software and hosting site for peer-reviewed conferences. In the process of uploading, additional information is entered along with the paper or project, including self-generated keywords. Each entrant provides a self-critical analysis of their work through the selection of several words or phrases that describe the ideas being explored in their investigations. Together, the aggregated texts and keywords form the primary database to operate upon.

The first step of the data analysis is to mine the compiled texts and keywords uncover quantitative patterns. The program was written in the open source platform Processing and was developed with reference to the work of Ben Fry, Craig Reynolds via Daniel Shiffman's, the Barbarian Group and John Carpenter. The applet developed for the exhibition design calculates the project position based on a 13+3 dimensional data set. The 13 dimensions of the information are based on relevant keywords and concepts uncovered from the current discourse of the ACADIA community while the +3 dimensions are qualitative values assigned by the curators. The quantitative list provides a survey of ideas, but remains reductive. Qualitative attributes relative to the theme of the conference, Affluence, Influence, and Confluence, are assigned by the curators to provide a critique of the compiled list of information and provides the ability for multi-value indexing of the lists.

Multi-dimensional data processing is similar to a joint study between researchers at Caltech and Cedars-Sinai. In "Visualizing Diffusion Tensor Images of the Mouse Spinal Cord," David Kremers worked with David H. Laidlaw, Eric T. Ahrens, and Carol Readhead to develop a software-based qualitative visualization method for the diagnosis of encephalitis in mice (a model for studying multiple sclerosis in humans) prior to the display of physical symptoms. The breakthrough of his work was his 4d+ model of 'dimensions of information,' which stated that any type of information can be composited into a traditional 2d or 3d picture plane in the same way that purely spatial information is modeled. Using a similar approach for the design of the exhibition, additional 15 dimensions of data provide opportunities to expose patterns of each of the project's relativity to the overall theme of the conference.

In order to populate the exhibition layout, the compiled keyword list was anchored in the gallery space according to relationships specified by the curators *(Figure 2)*. The intervention by the curator intentionally promotes curatorial critique through the exploration of possible relationships in a dynamic, fluid environment provided by the computational algorithm. Individual projects, however, are located based on their relationship to the 13 keywords and other 15 projects through a computational process of self-organization. The multi-dimensional keyword attributes provide the magnitude of the attraction and repulsion forces between the projects and the compiled keywords *(Figure 3)*. Thus, the individual projects are spatially located within the gallery by their magnetism relative to the information mined from the ACADIA community *(Figure 4)*.In addition to establishing spatial location, the additional (+3) values determine qualitative attributes such as radius, height, orientation, and color of the suspended cones displaying the individual projects *(Figure 5)*.

The development of this tool to assist in curatorial design and facilitate in the tri-phase transition from data to information to knowledge uncovers patterns of ideas that are current and relevant to the international ACADIA community. The process of collecting, data-mining, and critically filtering ideas Crowdsourced from a wide-area community through both computational methods and human intervention provide a multi-dimensional comparison of ideas that indicate and form the current discourse. Both the peer-reviewed and invited exhibitions are organized using the same method of relating individual projects to a single compiled database assembled from the ACADIA community. Utilizing the same process exposes different patterns of organization between the two exhibitions, comparing ideas being explored in practices located in New York for the invited exhibition to the ideas explored in the international peer-reviewer selected exhibition.

1   *"Project Report," Defense Advanced Research Projects Agency , accessed August 20, 2010, https://networkchallenge.darpa.mil/ProjectReport.pdf*

2   *Kremers, David. "Models of Weirdness", Artificial Natural Networks, p.6, De Verbeedling, Zeewolde, Netherlands, 2002.*

3   *Goodlett, James. "KEY PERFORMANCE INDICATORS: Moving Beyond Existing Opportunities" lecture at Refresh Savannah, Savannah, Georgia, February 16, 2010.*

4   *Howe, Jeff. "The Rise of Crowdsourcing," Wired Magazine, June 2006.*

5   *Fry, Ben. "Visualizing Data: Exploring and Explaining Data with the Processing Environment," Sebastopol, CA : O'Reilly Media, 2008.*

6   *Shiffman, Daniel. "The Nature of Code," ITP, Tisch School of the Arts, NYU 2008-2009 http://www.shiffman.net/teaching/nature/*

7   *The Barbarian Group, "Biomimetic Butterflies: A Generative Butterfly Installation on Display at the McLeod Residence", 2007, http://mcleodbutterflies.com/.*

8   *Carpenter, John. "Shoreline Equivalent: Qualitative Spaces in Interactive Art", Los Angeles, CA, UCLA, 2009.*

9   *Sprecher, Aaron. "Intensity, Extensity and Potentiality | A Few Notes on Information and the Architectural Organism", Second International Conference on Critical Digital, Proceedings, Harvard University GSD, Boston, 2009, pp. 109-118.*

10 *Laidlaw, David H., Ahrens, Eric T., Kremers, David., Readhead, Carol. "Visualizing Diffusion Tensor Images of the Mouse Spinal Cord." IEEE Visualization: Proceedings of the Conference on Visualization '98. Research Triangle Park, NC: October 18-23, 1998.*

Figure 1.

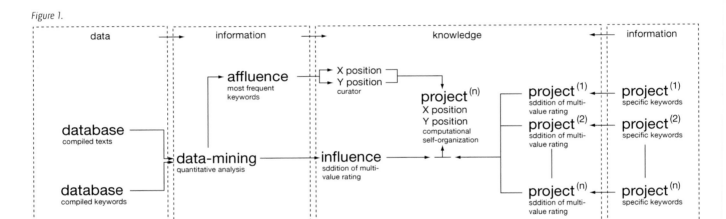

Figure 2.

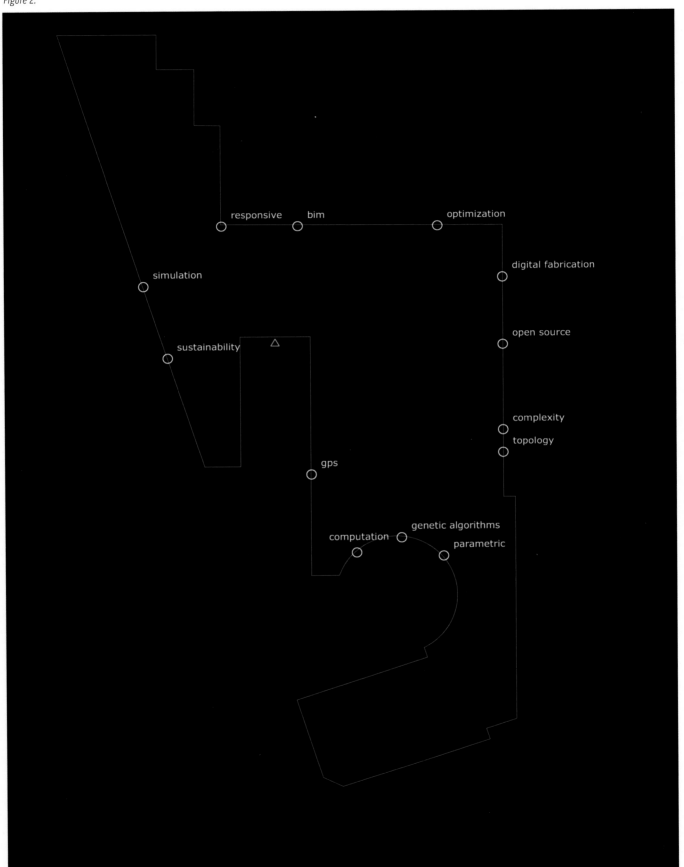

Figure 3.

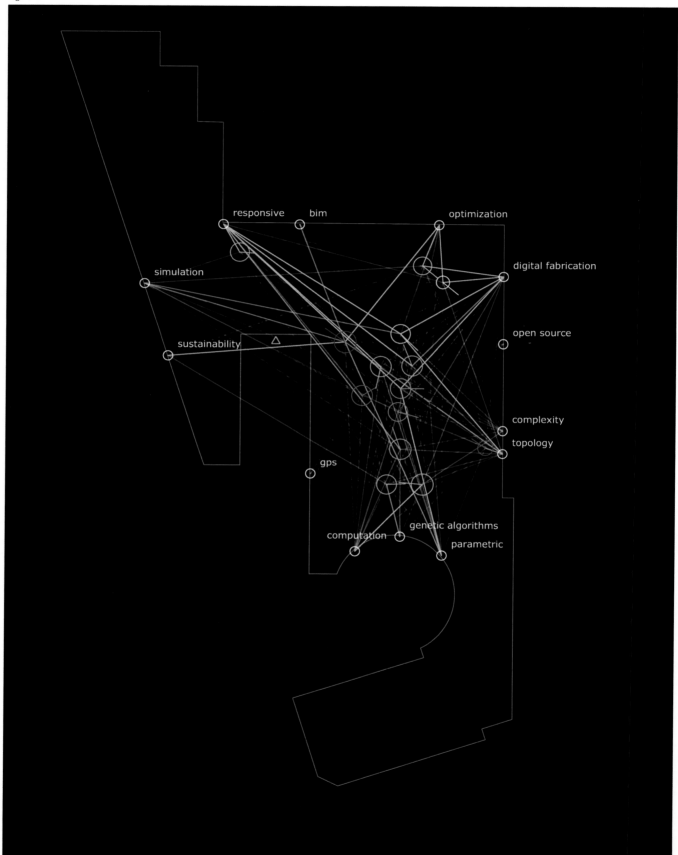

responsive   bim   optimization

simulation   digital fabrication

sustainability   open source

gps   complexity
                          topology

                          genetic algorithms
computation   parametric

Figure 4.

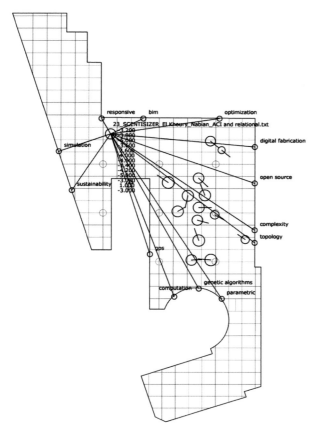

Figure 5.

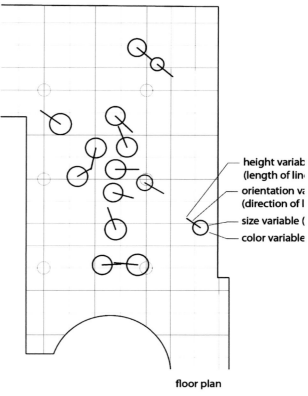

height variab
(length of lin
orientation v
(direction of l
size variable (
color variable

floor plan

Figure 5.

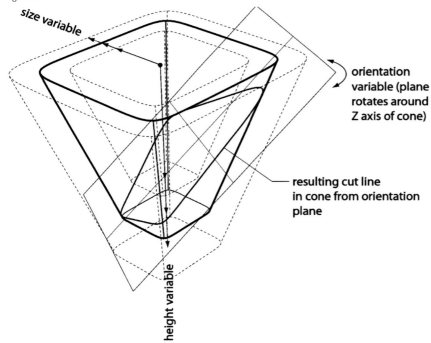

size variable

orientation
variable (plane
rotates around
Z axis of cone)

resulting cut line
in cone from orientation
plane

height variable

axonometric of typical cone

Curated Projects
The Saegel Gallery of The School of Architecture at The Pratt Institute

title: **Klex**

author: David Ruy, Karel Klein - Principals, Ruy Klein

Nicknamed "Klex" as a high school student for his love of making inkblots, Hermann Rorschach went on to develop a set of 10 klecksographies in his *Psychodiagnostik (1921)* as a tool for measuring an individual's psychological disposition. Though controversial, it is still widely used as a psychometric tool. As a device for initiating a controlled hallucination, the symmetrically reflected klex (stain) is devoid of meaning but capable of sustaining what seems to be an infinite range of projected meanings.

Taken as a compositional principle, klecksography provides an interesting model for examining the vague imbrications of sensation, perception, and conception in the architectural object. The fabrication experiments incorporate three compositional features from the klecksographic model. First is the incorporation of an extreme multiplicity of discrete surface elements. The elements vary in size, ranging from structural to ornamental capacities. Second, bilateral symmetry is used to provide figuration and consistency. Lastly, great attention is given to the finish of the surface. Luster, coloration, and reflectivity amplify the horizon of affects. Neither meaningful nor meaningless, the Klex is an apparatus for sensations.

The fabricated prototypes explore the bleeding edge of digital fabrication techniques. The large panel (Klex 1) experiments with adaptive tessellation techniques for CNC milling. Though CNC milling is now a fairly mature fabrication technology, the digital modeling techniques used for CNC output is still relatively undeveloped. Klex 1 incorporates a novel digital modeling procedure incorporating Subdivision Surfaces in the place of NURBS. Mesh files with extremely large polygon counts are extracted from Subdivision Surface models and are iteratively refined and conditioned through custom scripts. This shift in digital geometry allows for an efficient management of an extreme degree of intricacy impossible with NURBS geometry. In contrast to the digital modeling experiment of the large panel, the smaller blocks *(Klex 2, 3, & 4)*, experiment with processes of material formation. Though we have seen a rapid evolution of 3d-printing processes, applications have primarily been in the production of scaled prototypes. These prototypes are fabricated by EOS GmbH, a company pioneering the use of 3d-printing for manufacturing (moldless manufacturing). The blocks are 3d-printed in Alumide, a composite Aluminum-Nylon powder that is melted with a high energy laser. The Alumide material provides a high degree of compressive strength and unusual elastic properties. Conceived as digitally fabricated "bricks," the blocks are designed to tile seamlessly.

Credits

Ruy Klein: David Ruy, Karel Klein
EOS GmbH: Andrew Snow, Alex Dick
Parrish Industries: Drura Parrish, Rives Rash

Specifications

Klex 1
Dimensions: 4' (w) x 5' (h) x 4"(d) , CNC Milled High Density Foam, ChromaLusion Finish, Fabricated by Parrish Industries

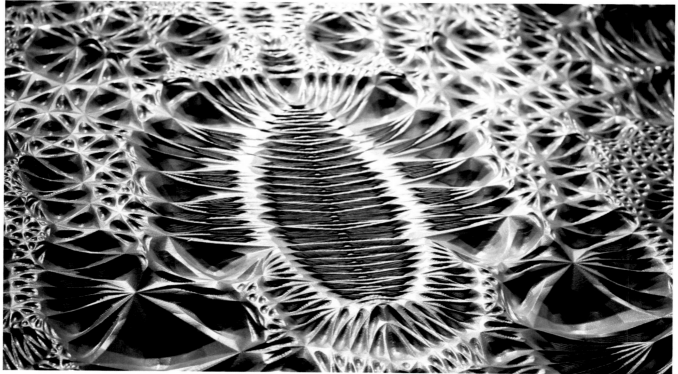

Klex 2, 3, & 4
Dimensions: 1'-3" (w) x 10" (h) x 3" (d), Alumide, Aluminum/Nylon composite, Silicone Finish, E-Manufactured on the EOS P 100

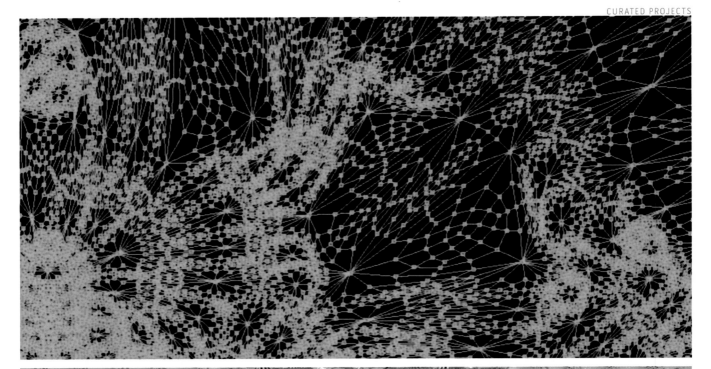

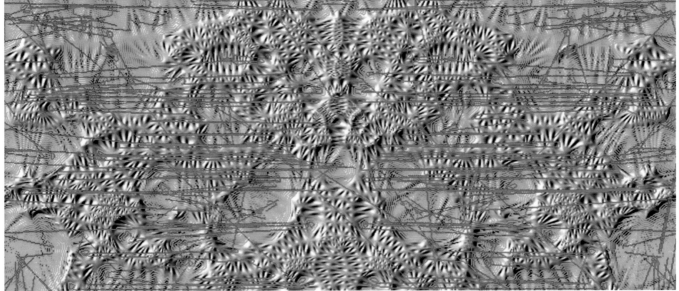

Credits: Ruy Klein: David Ruy, Karel Klein, EOS GmbH: Andrew Snow, Alex Dick, Parrish Industries: Drura Parrish, Rives Rash

title: **Baroque Parameters**

author: Andrew Saunders, Assistant Professor, Rensselaer Polytechnic Institute

"Though few modern scholars make use of the fact, or even seem to realize it, Baroque architecture was above all mathematical."
- George L. Hersey [1]

Scripting: the return of mathematical intuition

One of the most promising aspects of parametric design is that it promotes a distinct and disciplined bottom-up process of modeling geometry. A scripting based approach to parametric modeling utilizes features of programming within a native modeling environment. Geometry can then be generated by flow control (skipping and repeating lines) and variable control (logical and mathematical operations - data storage). [2] The ability to model with mathematical operations allows unprecedented accessibility to the generative possibilities and comprehension of equation based geometry.

Instrument for analysis

Recently, the opportunity arose to explore scripting as a tool for analyzing how geometry operates in Baroque architecture. Geometry and mathematics were integral to 17th-century science, philosophy, art, architecture and religion. It is what links Baroque architects Francesco Borromini and Guarino Guarini to other great thinkers of the period including Descartes, Galileo, Kepler, Desargues and Newton. [3] Plasticity and dynamism are explicit signatures of Baroque architecture. Less obvious are the disciplined mathematical principles which generate these effects.

Trigonometry through the Arc and the Chord

Borromini is often portrayed with traditional drawing tools of the 17th-century, the compass to draw an arc, and the ruler to draw a straight line or chord. In order to construct a square, 17th-century architects would first compose a governing circle and segment it with chords to constitute the four sides. [4] Geometry derived from this process is related by its association with a governing circle. As a result, triangle, circle or any equal sided polygon can be understood as parametric variations of each other.

To script these relationships, trigonometric functions are used to plot geometry by polar coordinates. [5] Trigonometry originated from chords. Ptolemy's Table of Chords was the most famous trigonometric table. Calculations used to solve for these chord lengths are equivalent to the modern sine function. [6] Through the exploitation of these ingrained trigonometric parameters, Baroque architects produced astonishing effects, performance, and continuity.

In Sant' Ivo , Borromini capitalizes on the verticality by transitioning parametrically from the most basic of polygons, at the base, two overlapping triangles to the infinite sided polygon, the circle. One can trace the movement downward from the chastity of forms in the heavenly zone to the increasing complexity of the earthly zone. [7] This continuous morphology from crude to smooth in turn initiates a novel structural performance. Because it cannot be reduced to a static element, the copula of Sant' Ivo avoids technical classification as a dome and is its own unique structure. [8]

In the Santissima Sindone, Guarini, uses a similar strategy to progress from a triangular base geometry and culminates in a kaleidoscope of hexagons. The staggering hexagons on the interior create an effect of perceptual psychology, fostering an illusion of extreme depth through telescoping vertical space. [9] The porosity of the nested geometry results in a relatively lightweight structural solution of an openwork dome and allows for the maximum light to penetrate the chasm below. A parametric model reveals that Guarini, integrates both structural performance and spatial effect through equation-based scalar and rotational operations.

Re-interpreting the Baroque

The analysis of the Baroque geometry was the initial starting point of the 2007 Rensselaer Rome Architecture Program that took as its premise "Re-Interpreting the Baroque". The studio went on to problematize the original parametric principles of the 17th Century with contemporary design parameters of performance and effect in the design of a Counter Reformation Art and Architecture Museum located in the historic center of Rome.

Endnotes
(1) George L. Hersey, Architecture and Geometry in the Age of the Baroque, University Of Chicago Press, (Chicago).p.4., (2) David Rutten, Rhinoscript101, Robert McNeel & Associates, 2007, p.4., (3) John Beldon Scott, Architecture for the Shroud: Relic and Ritual in Turin, University Of Chicago Press (Chicago) 2003, p.157., (4) Antonino Saggio (Re)searching and Redefining the content and Methods of Construction teaching in the new digital era, Eaae-Enhsa, Atene 2005 (isbn 2- 930301 25 2) pp. 13-34., (5) Jess Maertterer, Script to create nested regular polygons, Rhino 3DE Online Education, 2007, (6) Morris Kline, Mathematical Thought from Ancient to Modern Times (New York, Oxford University Press, 1972), p. 119-120., (7) Rudolf Wittkower, Art and Architecture in Italy 1600 to 1750, Penguin Books (Baltimore), 1958, p. 138, (8) Federico Bellini, Le cupole di Borromini. La "scientia" costruttiva in età barocca, Documenti di Architettura (Milano) 2004, p., (9) H.A. Meek, Guarino Guarini and His Architecture, Yale University Press (New Haven), 1988, P. 75

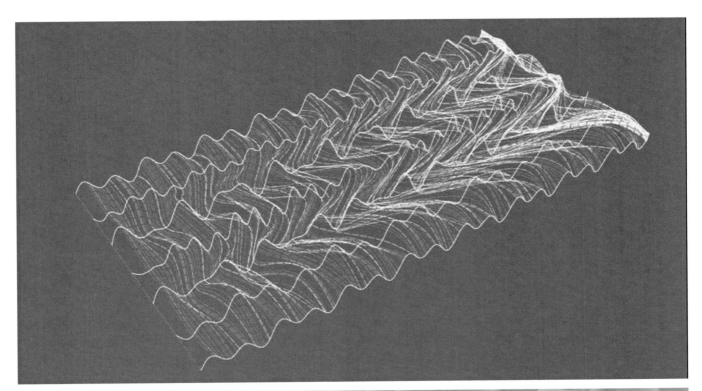

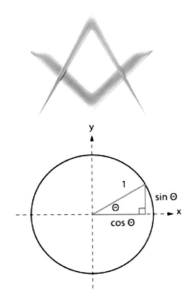

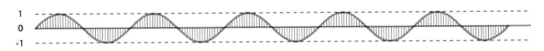

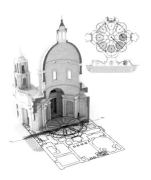

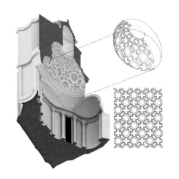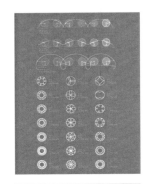

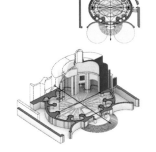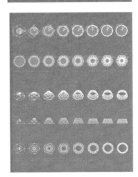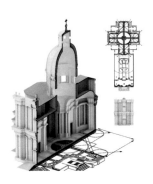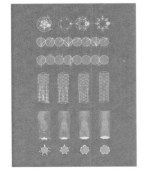

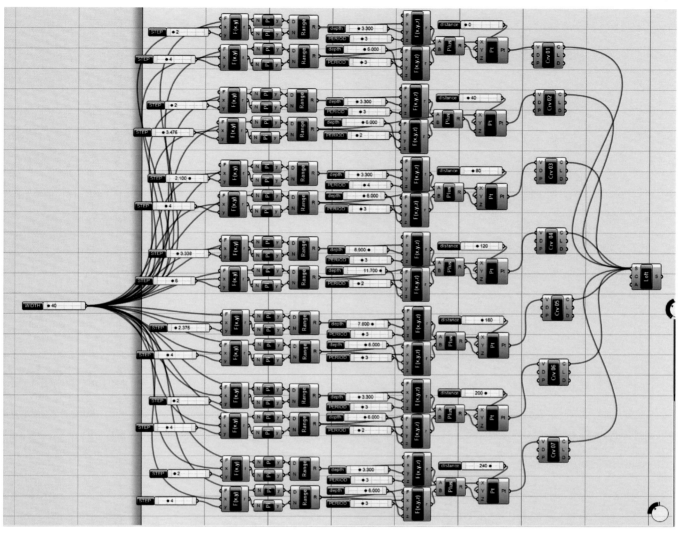

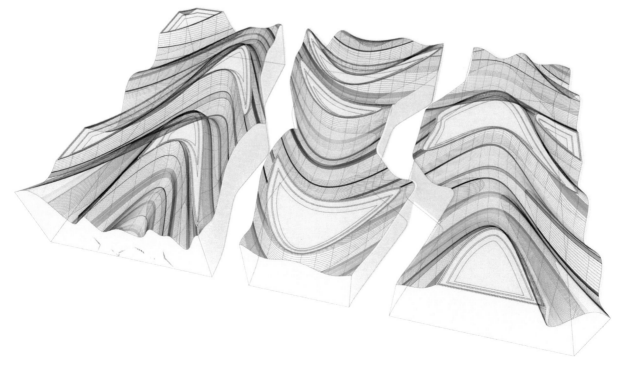

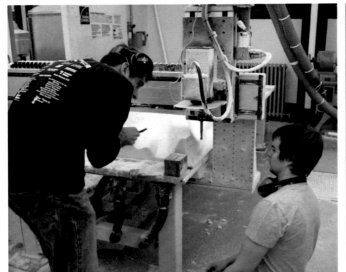

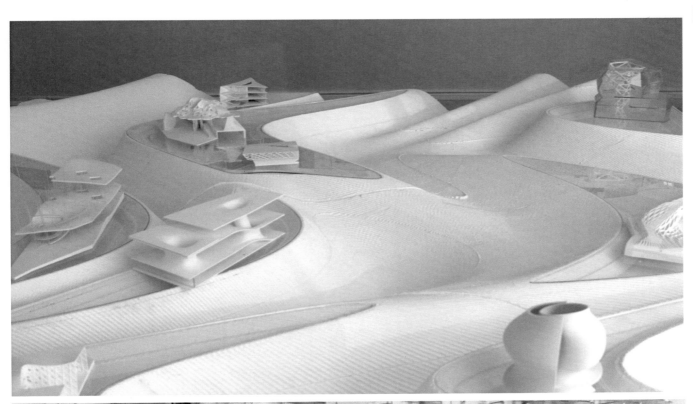

title:	**Pluripotent Design Strategies/PS_Canopy**
author:	Ferda Kolatan, Erich Schoenenberger, Principals, su11 architecture+design
design team:	*Richard Baxley, Hart Marlow*

Pluripotent: Not fixed as to developmental potentialities
- Dictionary.com

The evolution of form occurs through changes in development
- Sean B. Carroll

Pluripotent Structures describe a series of experimental investigations we have been conducting into more adaptive and variable design systems, which take advantage of multi-scalar and parametric techniques to generate formal organizations that challenge conventional architectural categorizations such as structure, volume and surface. Instead, these investigations focus on regionally customizable models, which maintain an overall design coherence while also displaying local specificity. Every one of these models has multiple potentialities and can be further refined through continuous feed-back loops. This approach is equally driven by the testing of unprecedented design methodologies as it is by the search for novel and exciting expressions in architecture. As many of the advanced computational techniques mature, more distinct and deliberate applications are necessary to examine the larger ramifications and effects of these prototypes.

PS_Canopy is one of these prototypes that have taken this investigation into a specific scale, program, and materiality. Taking cues from Biologist Sean B. Carroll's description of "Body Part" development in nature, PS_Canopy seeks to provide continual variations through the implementation of parametric dependencies. Carroll argues that any novelty of body-parts is based not on innovation but "rather a matter of modifying existing structures and of teaching old genes how to learn new tricks". These tricks, he reasons are achieved by switching on and off so-called tool-kit genes at different times and places through the course of cell development. If difference is created through a large number of combinatorial and incremental changes within a relatively manageable set of building blocks, a resourceful yet limitless design methodology can be formulated.

PS_Canopy operates on two distinct and growth based principles. The first one determines overall size, distribution, and density of the individual cellular components. The second one focuses on the internal transformation of these components into different performative parts. The canopy consists of three main parts, which in a morphological reference to flowers are called stem, petal, and leaf. The architectural definition of these translates into structure/post, shade, and seating/counter. The original parametric setup provides for a basic organization with latent possibilities to generate any number of stems, petals, and leafs in multiple scales with formal and functional variations. The model is open-ended as it can be adjusted and refined without its core constituents being altered.

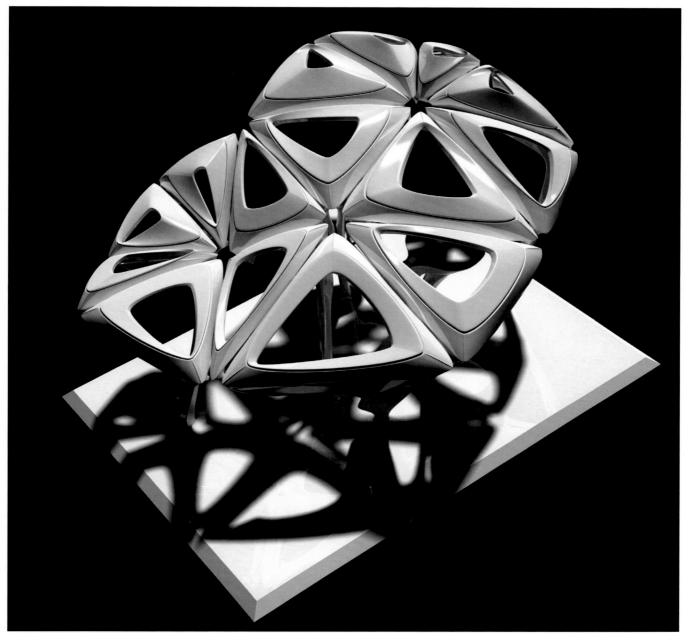

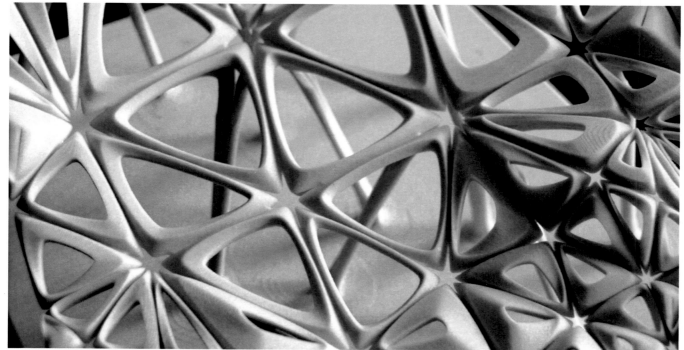

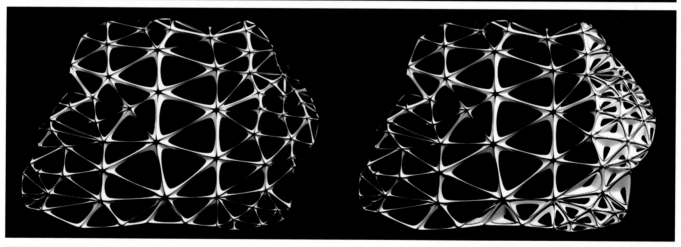

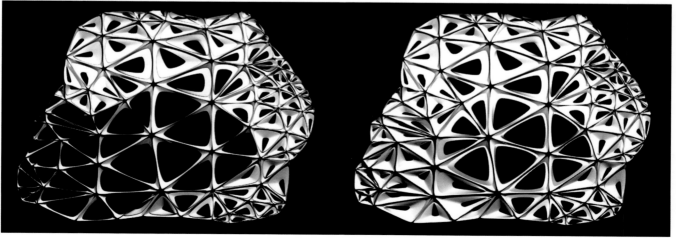

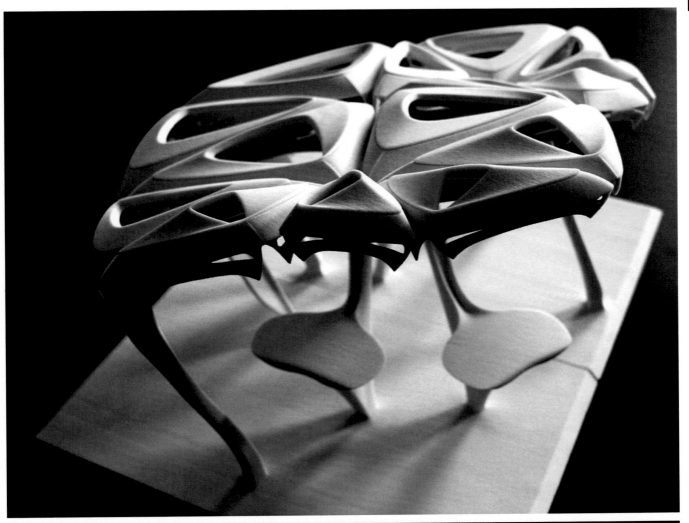

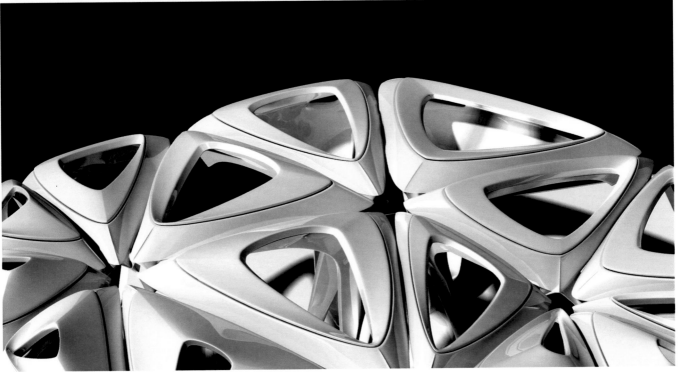

title: # Gravity Screens

author: Omar Khan, Associate Professor, University of Buffalo

Gravity Screens are surface constructions whose form results from gravity's effect on their material patterning. They are composed from elastomers of different Shore hardness that allow the screens to alter their shape horizontally, from flat to curved, and vertically from collapsed to extended. Rubber's elasticity and high weight to volume ratio make it problematic as a self-supporting material. However, the compounded effect of excessive weight on a stretchable material causes it to stiffen and hence become structured. This understanding became the basis for numerous experiments that explore the formal and material relations required to develop constructions that can move between mutable and stiff. Gravity, which is a relatively weak force, can be instrumentalized on such surfaces to give them a responsive form. This is done by using the weight of the rubber or added weights to induce a controlled stretch. In addition, by mixing hard and soft rubbers, the screens can calibrate their resistance to gravitational or motorized forces.

Material Compositions and Behaviors: In order to build with elastomers, one has to understand how to control their erratic behavior. In architecture this is primarily the role of geometry. But neither stereotomic nor tectonic geometrical composition, the most common methods in architecture, are suitable for this material. The most productive means for addressing stretching is an aperiodic geometric network. These are found in some fabric weaves but are pervasive in natural structures like radiolaria, bee hives, and coral. The aperiodic network can be simplified into nodes and vectors, where the nodes trace out a point cloud that gives the overall form, and the vectors connect the nodes to one another. While the network geometry provides an overall formal framework, it is the rendering of the nodes and vectors in elastomers of different Shore hardness that gives the structure its controlled kinetic behavior.

Material Computation: The possibilities provided by a mutable screen system are responsive and adaptable spaces that can mutate from circulation corridors to room clusters. This opens up unique possibilities for the inhabitation of crowds and collectives. We are exploring spaces of flow—where linear movements can easily be transformed into polar circulation. Likewise we are also looking at clustering geometries that allow the screens to transform from thresholds to enclosures. The mediation for such architecture requires an environmental sensing system that can measure the "energy" of a crowd. We are developing this by using sonar motes. In addition, the sequential motion of the screens is also being choreographed through computational means.

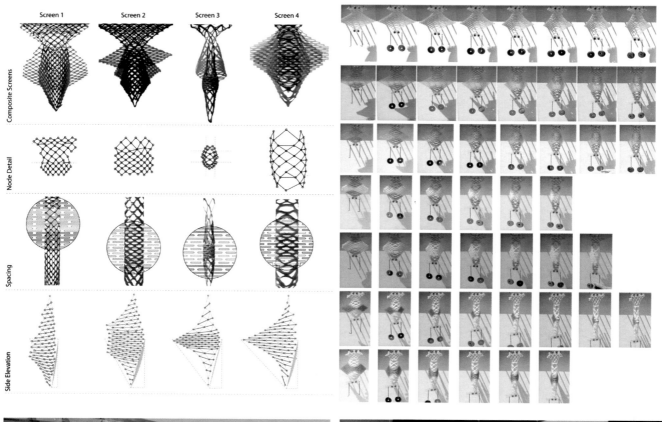

Composite Screens

Screen 1   Screen 2   Screen 3   Screen 4

Node Detail

Spacing

Side Elevation

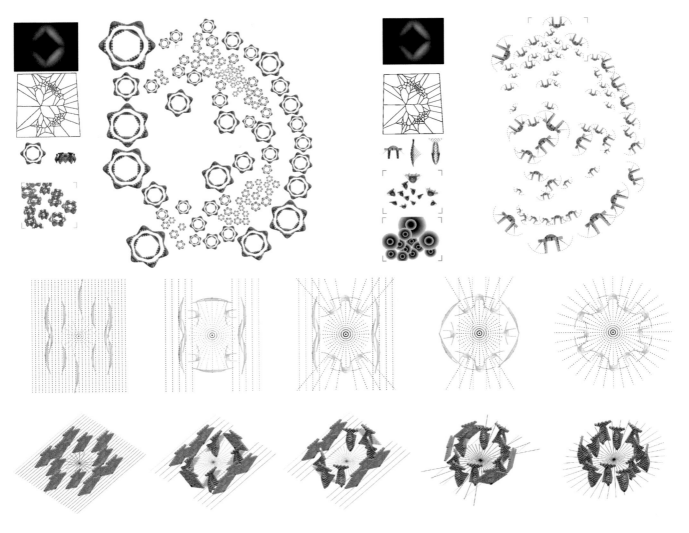

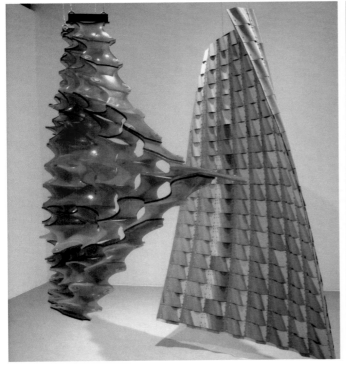

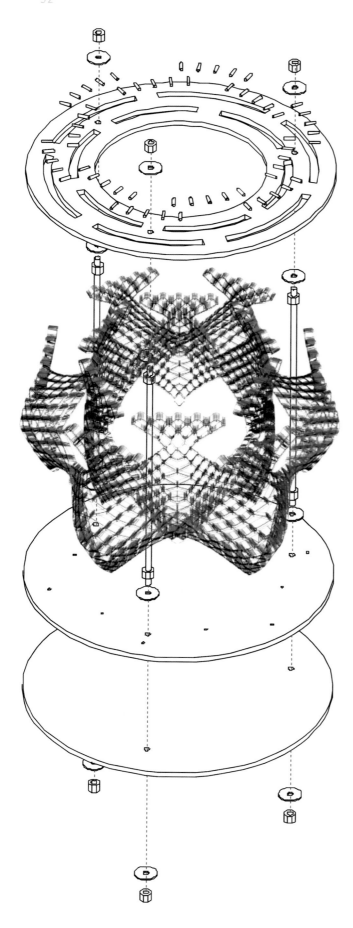

title: **Tactical Sound Garden [TSG]**

author: Mark Shepard, Assistant Professor, University of Buffalo

hyperlink: *www.tacticalsoundgarden.net*

The Tactical Sound Garden [TSG] is an open source software platform for cultivating public "sound gardens" in contemporary cities. It draws on the culture of urban community gardening to posit a participatory environment where new spatial practices for social interaction within technologically mediated environments can be explored and evaluated. Addressing the impact of mobile audio devices like the iPod, the project examines gradations of privacy and publicity within contemporary public space. Using a mobile device running TSG software, participants "plant" sounds within a positional audio environment. These plantings are mapped onto the coordinates of a physical location - overlaying a publicly constructed soundscape onto a specific urban space. Wearing headphones connected to a TSG enabled device, participants drift though virtual sound gardens as they move throughout the city.

Tactical Sound Gardens are by design underspecified with respect to both the content (sounds) and extent (geographic limits) of the urban sonic landscapes they enable. As the specific sounds, their playback parameters and geographic positions are determined by the participants and not the system's designer, gardens evolve over time through an iterative process that shifts the locus of a design practice from creating formal compositions of space and material to structuring interactions between people, wireless networks, digital sound objects, and urban topographies.

rhinoceros.mp3 | very loud | once a day | lat: 40.70851135 | lon: –73.99899292

runningBrook.mp3 | soft | once a minute | lat: 40.70851342 | lon: –73.99899010

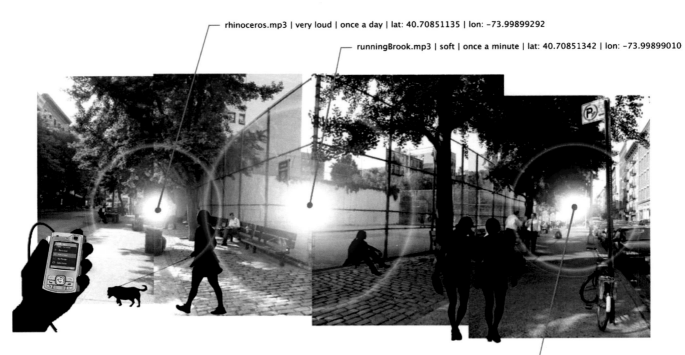

sayYes.mp3 | soft | once only | lat: 40.70851342 | lon: –73.99899010

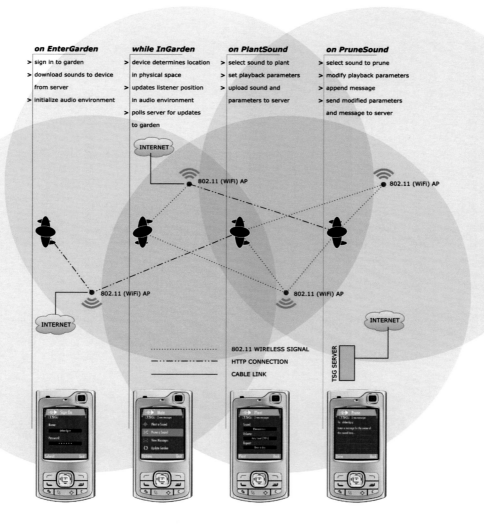

on EnterGarden
> sign in to garden
> download sounds to device from server
> initialize audio environment

while InGarden
> device determines location in physical space
> updates listener position in audio environment
> polls server for updates to garden

on PlantSound
> select sound to plant
> set playback parameters
> upload sound and parameters to server

on PruneSound
> select sound to prune
> modify playback parameters
> append message
> send modified parameters and message to server

INTERNET

802.11 (WiFi) AP

802.11 (WiFi) AP

802.11 (WiFi) AP

802.11 (WiFi) AP

INTERNET

INTERNET

TSG SERVER

802.11 WIRELESS SIGNAL
HTTP CONNECTION
CABLE LINK

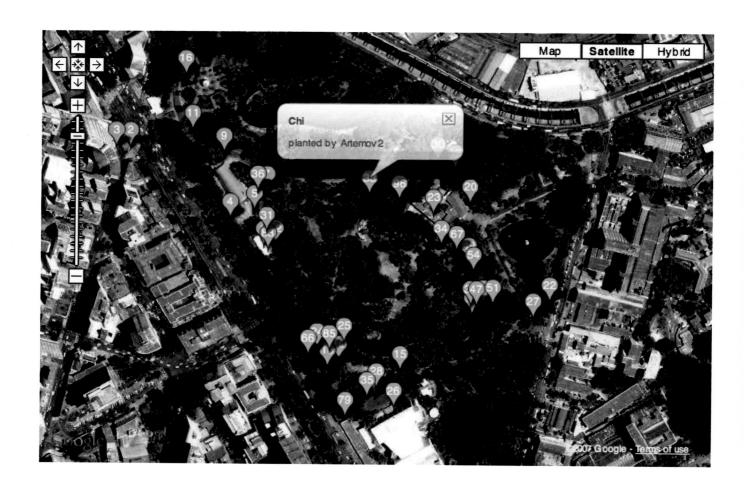

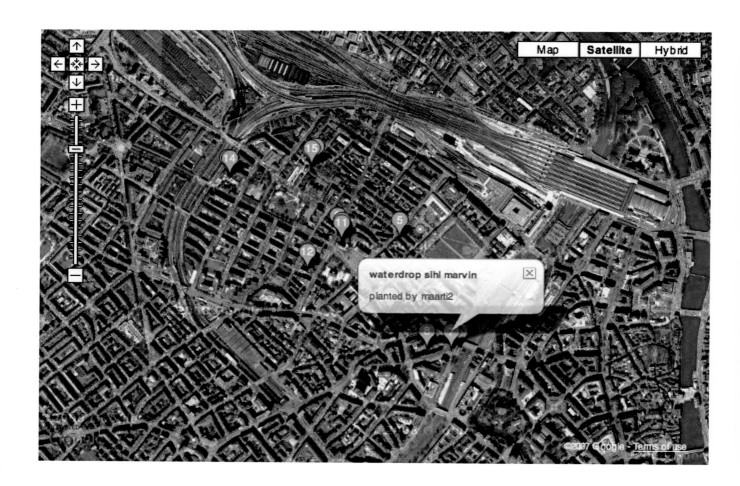

title: **Latent Figure Protocol**

author: Paul Vanouse, Associate Professor, University of Buffalo

A DNA fingerprint is often misunderstood by the lay public to be a single, unique human identifier. Its complex banding patterns imagined as an unchanging sentence written by mother nature herself that corresponds to each living creature. However there are hundreds of different enzymes that can be used to segment DNA and produce banding patterns. These patterns tell us as much about the enzyme as the subject that they appear to reproduce. Thus, the DNA gel image IS a cultural construct that is often naturalized.

Latent Figure Protocol uses DNA technologies to create images in which there is a tension between what is portrayed and the DNA used to make it. Each image is generated live in a performance context. Unlike a standard "DNA fingerprint", LFP uses DNA sequences chosen to create a recognizable image. Inserting DNA of known sizes into each lane of an electrophoresis gel allows a sequence of DNA bands to migrate at different speeds when voltage is applied, creating a 2-D grid of DNA bands resembling a low-res bitmap image.

Latent Figure Protocol takes the form of a media installation that uses DNA samples to create emergent representational images. The installation includes a live science experiment, the result of which is videotaped and repeated for the duration of the gallery exhibit. Employing a reactive gel and electrical current, Latent Figure Protocol produces images that relate directly to the DNA samples used. The above images were re-produced live. Each performance lasts approximately one hour, during which time audience members see the image slowly emerge.

In the first experiment, a copyright symbol is derived from the DNA of an industrially-produced organism (a plasmid called "pET-11a"), illuminating ethical questions around the changing status of organic life and the ownership of living organisms. Subsequent instances of the Latent Figure Protocol address other generic issues of organic life in the post-biological age: such as the "01" image to speak to the notion that "life is code".

The "wet-biological" techniques used in the Latent Figure Protocol were researched throughout 2006 and are based in restriction digestion of DNA samples and gel electrophoresis. The LFP imaging process relies upon knowing what size DNA is required for each band to move at the proper speed to make the correct image. This is essentially doing molecular biology IN REVERSE. Usually scientists use imaging techniques to determine an organism's genetic sequence, whereas Latent Figure Protocol utilizes known sequences in online databases to produce "planned" images.

These wet processes are consistent with my practice in emerging media forms. While I am deeply fascinated by many of these varied techno-scientific disciplines, I am interested in creatively "hacking" them with the aim of forcing the arcane codes of scientific meaning "to speak" in a broader cultural language.

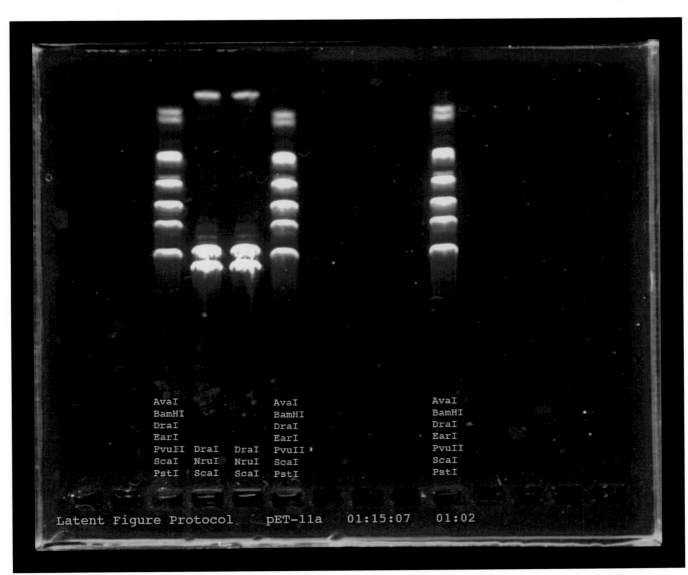

AvaI
BamHI
DraI
EarI
PvuII   DraI   DraI
ScaI   NruI   NruI
PstI   ScaI   ScaI

AvaI
BamHI
DraI
EarI
PvuII
ScaI
PstI

AvaI
BamHI
DraI
EarI
PvuII
ScaI
PstI

Latent Figure Protocol   pET-11a   01:15:07   01:02

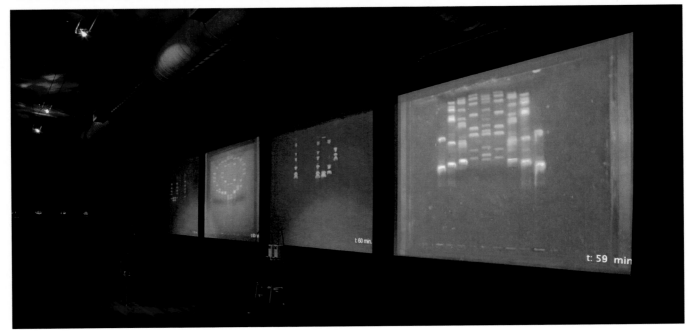

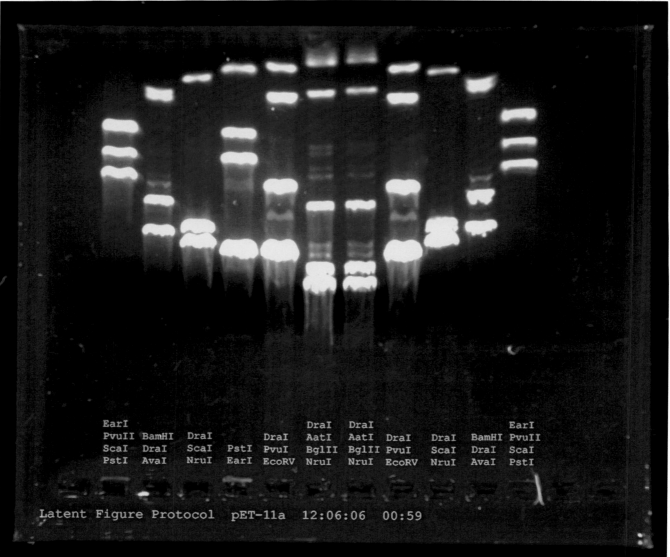

EarI					DraI	DraI				EarI
PvuII	BamHI	DraI		DraI	AatI	AatI	DraI	DraI	BamHI	PvuII
ScaI	DraI	ScaI	PstI	PvuI	BglII	BglII	PvuI	ScaI	DraI	ScaI
PstI	AvaI	NruI	EarI	EcoRV	NruI	NruI	EcoRV	NruI	AvaI	PstI

Latent Figure Protocol   pET-11a   12:06:06   00:59

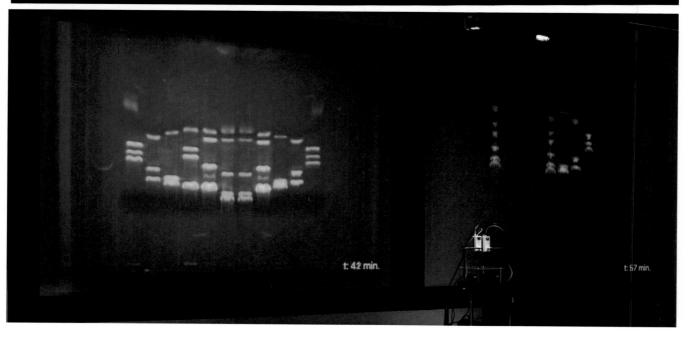

t: 42 min.   t: 57 min.

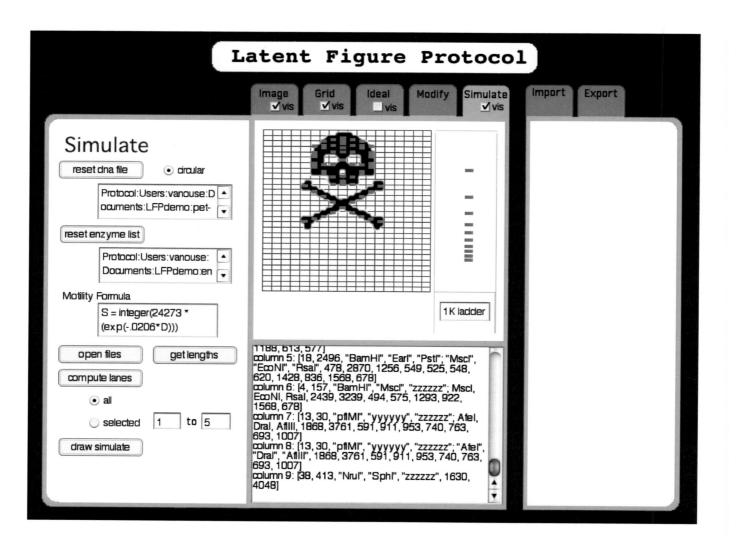

Latent Figure Protocol

Image [✓] vis   Grid [✓] vis   Ideal [ ] vis   Modify   Simulate [✓] vis   Import   Export

Simulate

reset dna file   (•) circular

Protocol:Users:vanouse:D
ocuments:LFPdemo:pet-

reset enzyme list

Protocol:Users:vanouse:
Documents:LFPdemo:en

Motility Formula

S = integer(24273 *
(exp(-.0206*D)))

open files   get lengths

compute lanes

(•) all

( ) selected   1 to 5

draw simulate

1K ladder

1188, 613, 577]
column 5: [18, 2496, "BamHI", "Earl", "PstI"; "MscI",
"EcoNI", "Rsal", 478, 2870, 1256, 549, 525, 548,
620, 1428, 836, 1568, 678]
column 6: [4, 157, "BamHI", "MscI", "zzzzzz"; MscI,
EcoNI, Rsal, 2439, 3239, 494, 575, 1293, 922,
1568, 678]
column 7: [13, 30, "pflMI", "yyyyyy", "zzzzzz"; Afel,
DraI, AflIII, 1868, 3761, 591, 911, 953, 740, 763,
693, 1007]
column 8: [13, 30, "pflMI", "yyyyyy", "zzzzzz"; "Afel",
"DraI", "AflIII", 1868, 3761, 591, 911, 953, 740, 763,
693, 1007]
column 9: [38, 413, "NruI", "SphI", "zzzzzz", 1630,
4048]

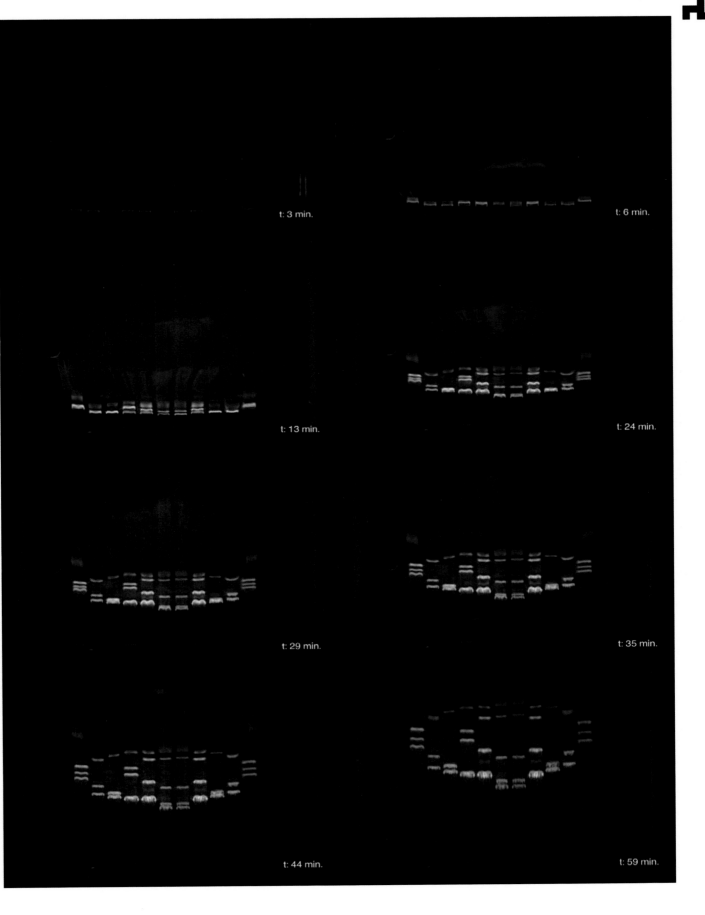

t: 3 min.

t: 6 min.

t: 13 min.

t: 24 min.

t: 29 min.

t: 35 min.

t: 44 min.

t: 59 min.

title: **R.V.**

author: Michael Meredith, Hilary Sample, Principals, MOS

The Beaux-arts pedagogy so deeply impressed a two-dimensional model of composition on architecture that we continue to largely rely on orthographic plans and elevations today. Their abstract representational conventions presented complexity in terms of proportion, symmetry, axes, figures, grids, repetition, poché, and scale, confining the routines of architectural thought to the formal arrangements of part-to-whole. The flattening of our world was of course encouraged over time because it allowed architectural designs to achieve portability and operational efficiency. It was the primary medium of architecture. Importantly, it produced a mechanical datum—a playing field—in which all buildings could be evaluated against each other.

This abstraction initially allowed architectural designs to be exchanged in the same way as paintings: compositional imagery which encouraged and illustrated discourse. The de-skilling of the Beaux-arts plans into reductive diagrams as the generators of design strategies has further detached representation from the material configurations they organize. Coupled with the rise of photographic realism as the means of blogged and googled architectural discourse, this procedure has shifted the discipline toward a more diffuse relationship with its representational medium.

Computational tools have allowed architects to grasp and articulate data in ever-expanding ways. Previous generations of architects used digital technology to examine design as three-dimensional form and complex spatial geometry. This residual formal emphasis projected the Beaux Arts two-dimensional discourse into the third and fourth dimensions without questioning the premise of architecture's formal-painterly bias in relation to other flows and forces. At MOS, we are interested in using the diffusion of representation allowed by computation to reexamine the social, cultural, political, and economic bandwidth of architectural activity. Our work aims to shift what has been an inward art-historical discourse of composition and formlessness, towards a fuller consideration of structure, weight, balance, friction, and materiality, not in order to reconstitute an 'authentic' humanist endeavor, but as a way of fundamentally rethink modes of 'composing.'

The design process has ceased to be solely based upon hyberbolic anxieties of form, where avant-garde practices must constantly seek new means of escape from previous status quo methodologies. Today architecture must enter larger contests that treat software as a necessary tool for constructing new futures rather than a purely visual novelty. Previous generations of architects had to choose between Art and Life, representation or realism, which we believe is a false choice and no longer relevant given our diffused immersion in media. The distinction between art and life or autonomy and heteronomy is no longer clear-cut, but rather flattened into this new territory in which we work. Developing software environments permits us to continue the avant-garde mandate of formal experimentation, conjuring new means of organizing matter that is neither purely craft nor composition, but both simultaneously.

In order to do this, we write our own software in Processing, utilizing real time physics engines that are typically from the video gaming industry. This allows us to do approximated structural testing, to set up a world of forces with rigid and soft body collision detection. Within this alternative environment, that oscillates between reality and fiction, we can play and iterate designs. Our work is not about optimization, rather playing. We are not engineers. Our work, although utilizing aspects of engineering and construction, is about architecture.

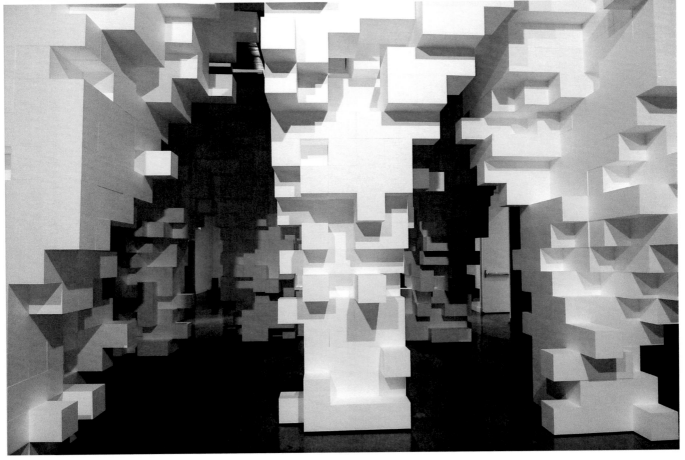

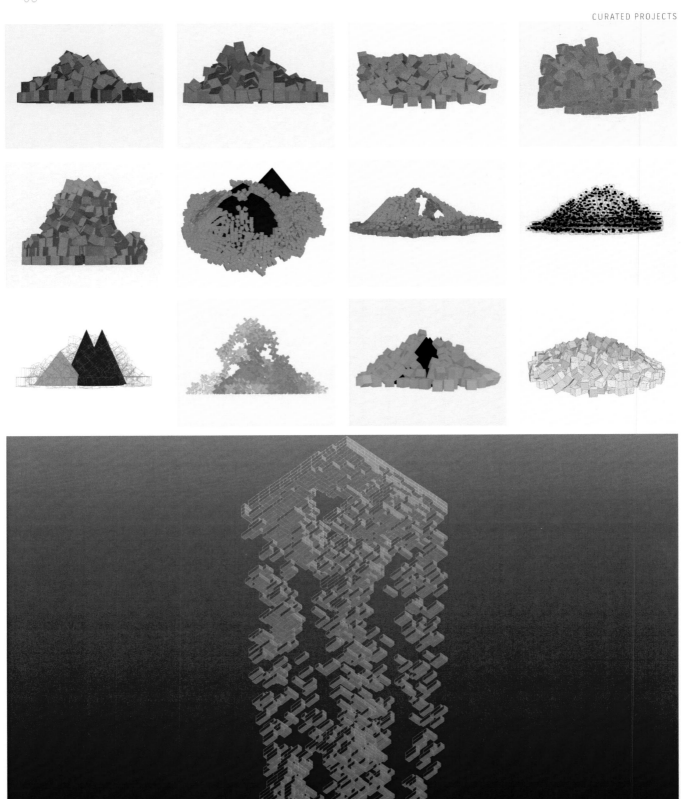

life in:formation

title: **Onondaga Creek Project**

author: Mark Linder, Julia Czerniak, Associate Professors, Syracuse University
McLain Clutter, Assistant Professor, University of Michigan

This transdisciplinary project proposes that Geographic Information Systems can be converted into a productive tool for architecture and urban design by developing innovative urban modeling techniques using commonly available census and municipal data. Now ubiquitous in urban planning and real-estate development, GIS most commonly uses spatio-demographic data to validate or reify conventional planning practices. This project exploits the ubiquity of GIS by converting data-sets with discrete categories and boundaries into pliable and fluid relational topologies. These manipulations of spatial data explore the proposition that models for describing and understanding web-based virtual communities are also useful for describing the potential organization of communities in actual, urban space. We propose that when these topologies are superimposed on conventional plans or maps, they suggest new kinds of densities, intensities, gaps, territories, and latent communities in cities—deeply implicating design strategies for repurposing or modifying existing infrastructure and incentivizing the development of properties.

The Onondaga Creek Project identifies latent communities and underutilized properties that exist in proximity to a neglected but important element of infrastructure and landscape in a typical shrinking city. GIS is used to correlate the spatial organization of latent communities and dormant properties that might anchor these communities and to propose design strategies focused on sustainable development through land banking, environmental remediation, and the linking of educational and recreational facilities. Ultimately, the aim is to propose unprecedented forms of urbanism that might emerge in cities of declining density and increasing diversity.

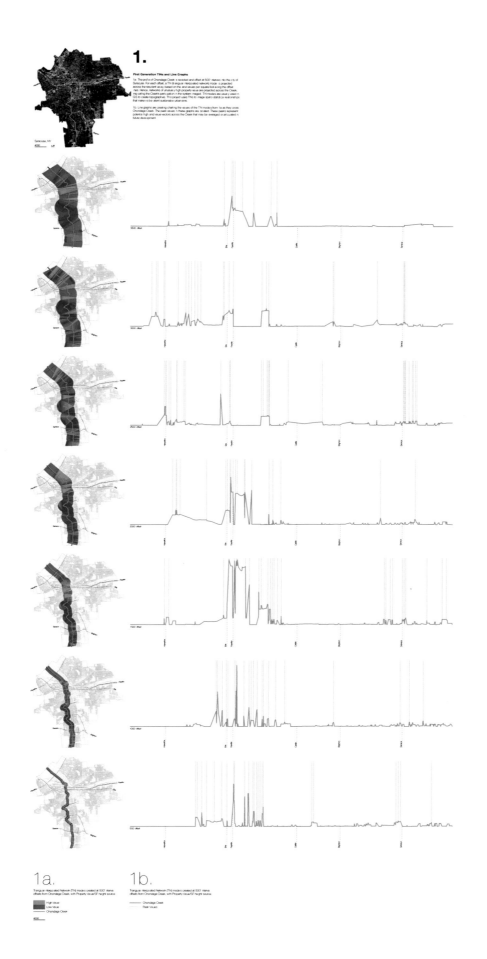

1.

First Generation TINs and Line Graphs

1a. The profile of Onondaga Creek is selected and offset at 500' interves into the city of Syracuse. For each offset, a TIN (triangular interpolated network) model is projected across the resultant valley, based on the land values per square foot along the offset net. Hence, networks of unusual y high property value are projected across the Creek, mapping the Creek's participation in the system mapped. TIN models are usua y used in GIS to create topographies. This project uses This to image spatio-statistical relationships that make visible latent sustainable urbanisms.

1b. Line graphs are created charting the values of the TIN models from 1a as they cross Onondaga Creek. The peak values in these graphs are scaled. These peaks represent potential high and value vectors across the Creek that may be averaged or articulated in future development

1a.

Triangular Interpolated Network (TIN) models created at 500' interve offsets from Onondaga Creek, with Property Value/SF height source

▉ High Value
▨ Low Value
— Onondaga Creek

1b.

Triangular Interpolated Network (TIN) models created at 500' interve offsets from Onondaga Creek, with Property Value/SF height source

— Onondaga Creek
— Peak Values

2.

Peak Value Vectors

1a. The peak property value vectors, located in 1b are grafted back on to the ink-blots

1b. The Peak Value vectors are calculated with the demographic data pertaining to the and zones per square foot height sound.

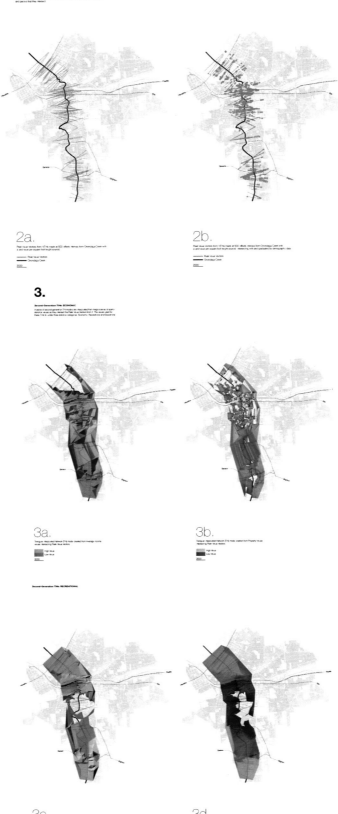

2a.
Peak Value Vectors from 1/2 ha made at 500 offsets. Interval from Onondaga Creek with a and zone per square foot height sound.

— Peak Value Vectors
▬ Onondaga Creek

2000

2b.
Peak Value vectors from 1/2 ha made at 500 offsets. Interval from Onondaga Creek with a and value per square foot height sound. interacting with and graduated by demographic data

— Peak Value Vectors
▬ Onondaga Creek

2000

3.

Second-Generation Title: ECONOMIC

A series of second-generation TIN models are disaggregated then maps a series of super-distortive values as they interact the Peak Value Vectors from 2. The values used to these TINs to under three distinct categories: Economic, Recreational and Educational.

3a.
Triangular Irregulated Network (TIN) made created from Average income values interacting Peak Value Vectors

■ High Value
□ Low Value

2000

3b.
Triangular Irregulated Network (TIN) made created from Property Values values interacting Peak Value Vectors

■ High Value
□ Low Value

2000

Second-Generation Title: RECREATIONAL

3c.
Triangular Irregulated Network (TIN) made created from Recreational Expense values interacting Peak Value Vectors

■ High Value
□ Low Value

2000

3d.
Triangular Irregulated Network (TIN) made created from Bike Ownership values interacting Peak Value Vectors

■ High Value
□ Low Value

2000

Second-Generation TINs: EDUCATIONAL

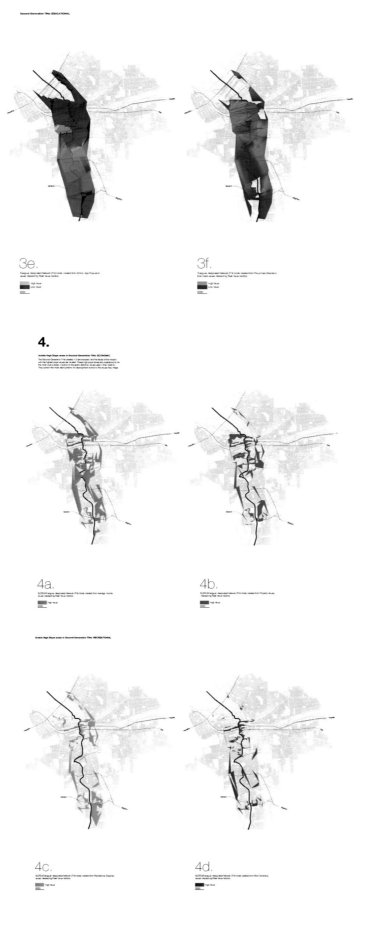

3e.

Triangular Interpolated Network (TIN) node created from School Age Population values intersecting Peak Value Vectors

High Value
Low Value

3f.

Triangular Interpolated Network (TIN) node created from Pre-primary Education Enrollment values intersecting Peak Value Vectors

High Value
Low Value

4.

Isolate High Slope areas in Second-Generation TINs: ECONOMIC

The Second-Generation TINs created in 3 are annotated and the areas of the nodes with the highest slope values are isolated. These high-slope areas are understood to be the most volatile areas in relation to the spatial statistical values used in their creation. They contain the most salient patterns for development evolve in the values they integrate.

4a.

SLOPE of Triangular Interpolated Network (TIN) node created from Average rooms values intersecting Peak Value Vectors

High Value

4b.

SLOPE of Triangular Interpolated Network (TIN) node created from Property values intersecting Peak Value Vectors

High Value

Isolate High Slope areas in Second-Generation TINs: RECREATIONAL

4c.

SLOPE of Triangular Interpolated Network (TIN) node created from Recreations Expense values intersecting Peak Value Vectors

High Value

4d.

SLOPE of Triangular Interpolated Network (TIN) node created from Site Ownership values intersecting Peak Value Vectors

High Value

Isolate High Slope areas in Second-Generation Title: EDUCATIONAL

4e.

SLOPE of Fatigue-reoccupated Network (THd node created from School Age Population issues reoccurring Peak Value Vectors)

High Value

2000

4f.

SLOPE of Fatigue-reoccupated Network (THd node created from Pre-primate Education Enrollment issues reoccurring Peak Value Vectors)

High Value

2000

5.

Hybrid Voids

The vand parcels of the city that are either Vacant or only Tax Delinquent or of very Low Land Value (LV4 000) are located. Where these parcels are adjacent to one another they are joined into one large parcel. Then a combined parcels or greater that 40 000 square feet are located. These parcels are sufficient size to host large public or private development that might indicate future alternative.

5a.

A Vacant properties

Vacant Property

Onondaga Creek

2000

5b.

A Tax Delinquent properties

Tax Delinquent Property

Onondaga Creek

2000

5c.

+ Vacant properties

Low Value Property

Onondaga Creek

2000

5d.

= Tax Delinquent properties, Vacant Properties and Low Value Properties with a continuous area of over 40 000 sf

Tax Delinquent Property   Low Value Property   Onondaga Creek

> 40 000sf

2000

6.

Interwort Voids and Slopes

The High Slope areas scaled 1-4 are layered and overlayed with the Hybrid Voids scaled 0-9. Where the paired High Slope area 1 the Hybrid points a sustainable urban programs and development strategies are suggested.

7.

Zoned for new Sustainable Urbanisms

The city is re-zoned to encourage development that will concretized the latent communities implicated in the GIS analysis. Zoned urban developments enroll both private and public interests, and include both top-down regulations and bottoms-up emergent urbanisms.

Legend

Vacant, Delinquent or Low Value properties to be land-banked and re-purposed as public space. Incentivized TDR's from center of region to periphery. Phased environmental remediation of available properties immediately adjacent to Creek.

Vacant, Tax Delinquent or Low Value Properties.

Tax incentives for charter school development, zoned for mixed-income residential development proximate to schools.

Vacant, Tax Delinquent or Low Value Properties that could be immediately re-purposed as charter schools.

Tax abated commercial and office development. Special development area for technology and knowledge-based industries.

Vacant, Tax Delinquent or Low Value Properties to be land-banked and gifted to technology or knowledge-based corporations.

Incentives for bicyclist facilities in development. Public bike rental Kiosks.

New Bike Lanes

Zoned for public and private sports facilities.

Vacant, Tax Delinquent or Low Value Properties that could be immediately re-purposed as public or private sports facilities.

Mega churches, community centers, field houses, cultural facilities.

Vacant, Tax Delinquent or Low Value Properties that could be immediately re-purposed as mega-churches, community centers, field houses, cultural facilities.

Tax incentives for chartered pre-primary school development and day-care facilities. Subsidized residential development proximate to schools.

Vacant, Tax Delinquent or Low Value Properties that could be immediately re-purposed for chartered pre-primary school development and day care facilities.

2000'

title: **Aortic Arc**

author: David Herd, Principal, Buro Happold

The Aortic Arc is the result of a linked set of developments at two different scales: the macro scale of the overall form and the micro scale of the component. The work flow followed a process of speculation and testing through physical and digital analysis in specific stages: form finding, component design, non-linear structural analysis, design optimization, and fabrication.

Form Investigation and Component Design

An overall shape which fit the constraints of the site was developed using AutoCAD for the existing context, Form-Z nurb surfaces to work out the canopy design, and Pepakura to make physical paper models to test fit and concept. The next step in the work flow was to analyze the individual component and identify materials and joinery for fabrication. This step started with physical paper models which were then turned into digitally scripted manipulated surfaces using Rhino and Generative Components. A Rhino script was used to turn the 3D forms into 2D AutoCAD drawings which could then drive a laser cutter to make the parts.

Non-Linear Analysis: Structural Engineering

From the engineering side of the project, CATIA was used to model the building structure and approximate the surface. CATIA's parametric drivers allowed visualizing and quickly adjusting the surface and rings locations to avoid interference with the building structure.

Once the geometry was established in CATIA, the boundary conditions were imported (the rings) and a form-finding exercise in Tensyl begun. This model and methodology resulted in minimal surface for these boundary conditions, and allowed the upper rings to shift into the proper location to create a catenary-like. Next, the geometries were exported from Tensyl into Robot, and the system was analyzed as a cable net model. The lower hoop was released, and the entire surface was allowed to deflect and shear as necessary. The surface deflected slightly, but overall experienced little change from the initial Tensyl model. Finally, the surface was analyzed with Robot using panel elements to model the HDPE surface. The stresses were estimated in the surface and were determined if there would be any unacceptable concentrations of planar or shear stresses in the relatively rigid surface. In these final models the surface showed very minimal bending and a smooth distribution of stresses well below the limits of the material.

Design Optimization

The final design included optimization of the component's shape to allow for more or less light and views from above. Generative Components allowed us to create a gradient in the size of the aperture of each component. It also allowed to vary the height and direction of the scooped portion of each component.

Fabrication

The last step in the work flow was turning the final design into a set of parts which could be manufactured. A Rhino script was run on the entire assembly to label each component uniquely and locate the attachment points between each piece. A final Rhino script was run to unfold each piece into a 2D pattern nesting the pieces into panels. The 2D drawing was used as the final approved shop drawing which drove the CNC milling machine used by the steel fabricator.

Credits
Architect:
Visible Research Office
Mark L. Donohue, AIA – Principal
Americo A Diaz-O – Project Architect
Charles Lee – Project Designer, Renderings
Chris Chalmers – Component Design & Scripting
Jason Chang – Component Design & Scripting

Engineer:
Greg Otto – Principal
Ron Elad – Project Manager
Tom Reiner– Project Engineer, Non-linear Analysis
Yukie Hirashima – Complex Geometry Modeling
Krista Flascha – Technical Designer

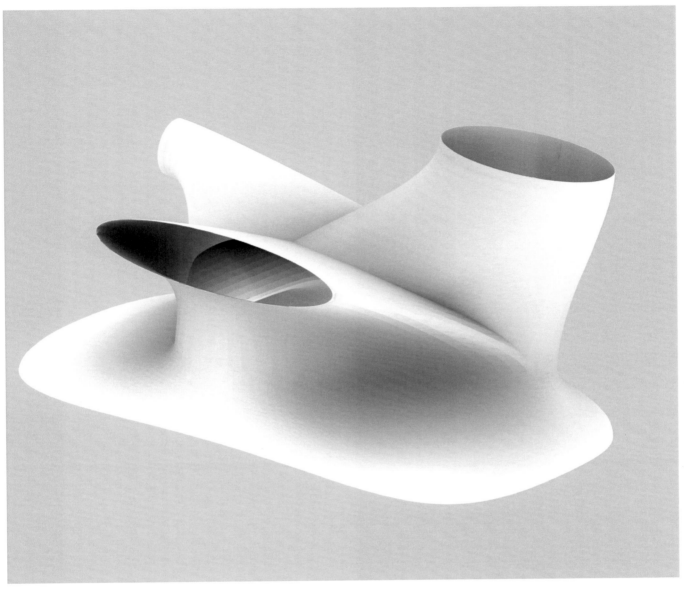

3D digital model to find form in Form-Z
Site visit to get field measurements

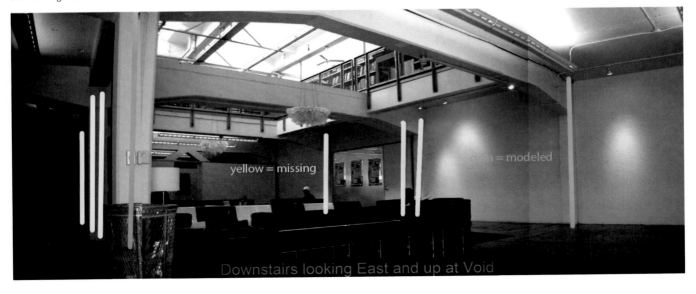

yellow = missing   green = modeled

Downstairs looking East and up at Void

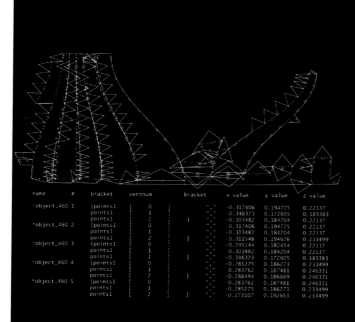

name	#	bracket	vertnum	bracket	x value	y value	z value
*object_460	1	{points1	[0]		","	-0.317406	0.194775	0.22137
		points1	[1]		","	-0.348373	0.172605	0.183383
		points1	[2]	}	","	-0.303482	0.184204	0.22137
*object_460	2	{points1	[0]		","	-0.317406	0.194775	0.22137
		points1	[1]		","	-0.303482	0.184204	0.22137
		points1	[2]	}	","	-0.311548	0.194676	0.233499
*object_460	3	{points1	[0]		","	-0.295144	0.182454	0.22137
		points1	[1]		","	-0.303482	0.184204	0.22137
		points1	[2]	}	","	-0.348373	0.172605	0.183383
*object_460	4	{points1	[0]		","	-0.285275	0.186273	0.233499
		points1	[1]		","	0.283762	0.187481	0.246331
		points1	[2]	}	","	-0.288494	0.186669	0.246331
*object_460	5	{points1	[0]		","	-0.283762	0.187481	0.246331
		points1	[1]		","	-0.285275	0.186273	0.233499
		points1	[2]	}	","	-0.273107	0.192653	0.233499

name	#	bracket	vertnum	bracket	x value	y value	z value
*object_460	1	{points1	[0]		","	-0.317406	0.194775	0.22137
		points1	[1]		","	-0.348373	0.172605	0.183383
		points1	[2]	}	","	-0.303482	0.184204	0.22137
*object_460	2	{points1	[0]		","	-0.317406	0.194775	0.22137
		points1	[1]		","	-0.303482	0.184204	0.22137
		points1	[2]	}	","	-0.311548	0.194676	0.233499
*object_460	3	{points1	[0]		","	-0.295144	0.182454	0.22137
		points1	[1]		","	-0.303482	0.184204	0.22137
		points1	[2]	}	","	-0.348373	0.172605	0.183383
*object_460	4	{points1	[0]		","	-0.285275	0.186273	0.233499
		points1	[1]		","	-0.283762	0.187481	0.246331
		points1	[2]	}	","	-0.288494	0.186669	0.246331
*object_460	5	{points1	[0]		","	-0.283762	0.187481	0.246331
		points1	[1]		","	-0.285275	0.186273	0.233499
		points1	[2]	}	","	-0.273107	0.192653	0.233499

Pepakura 3D Conversion of Computer Model

Study Model

Initial coordination between architect and engineer
Continuous work in Form Z to find the desired aesthetics
Initial panel design and instantiation in Generative Components
Pepkura used to create physical paper models

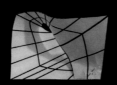

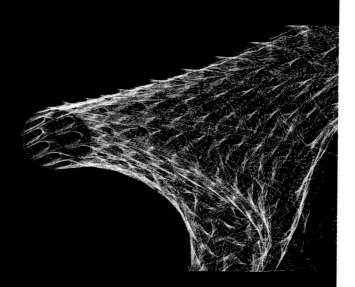

Generative Components

Wireframe View of Panelized System

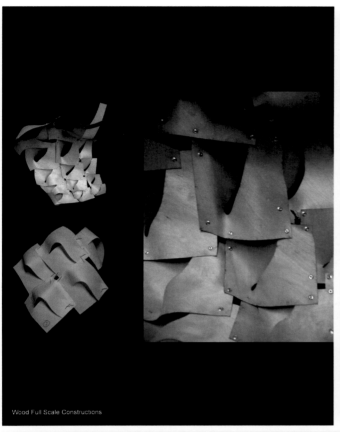

Wood Full Scale Constructions

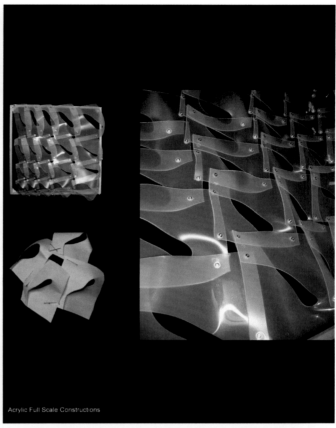

Acrylic Full Scale Constructions

1:1 scale mockup – testing different HDPE
3D Studio Max used to visualize final design

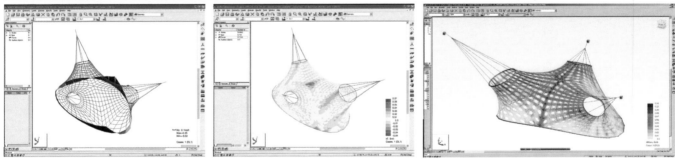

*The whole design team is meeting for the first time: understanding
the structural behavior of the surface
Analysis in Tensyl
Analysis in ROBOT*

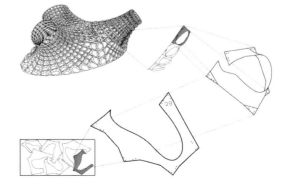

Up in the air – fully installed

title: **Evolution of Virtual Form**

author: Jesse Reiser, Nanako Umemoto, Principals, Reiser + Umemoto

When considering the diagrid concrete shell's evolution from O-14 to Shenzhen T3, one must first consider the move from masonry logics of building to those of vector based construction. The shift from arch-and-wall ideas to column-and-beam signifies a shift in thinking about matter, in which structural logics within building components gradually become freed from the 'excessive' material surrounding them. The development of this idea leads to analysis of ideal structural form—the evolution of the cable and point load, and on to the truss and space frame, etc.—which is the logical extension of the machine-aesthetic, the Modern concept of Functionalism, and its eventual degradation into baleful high-tech.

In the case of O-14, a 22-story office tower in Dubai, typical high-tech tower building systems were immediately determined to be unsuitable for the project, so instead of proliferating a conventional column and slab structure with a curtain wall, the building was literally turned inside out and the structure was developed as an exoskeleton. Various tower shapes were studied in addition to several pattern organizations, and feedback from both the client and structural engineers guided the manipulation of the overall tower form, as well as the determination of the patterns of openings. The final iteration is a fine-tuned combination of a structural branching pattern, turbulence field, and porosity gradients. Modulation of this pattern works like camouflage becoming disruptive and de-materializing the tower block. The shell's pattern changes as its relationship to the viewer changes, and in conjunction with additional patterns of light and shadow, produces a sort of 'virtual form.'

The shell of Shenzhen T3, an airport terminal in Shenzhen, China, is similar to O-14, in that its efficiency is tied to a system of mass-customized formwork, used to produce a continuous variation of openings. In the case of O-14, because of the advantages of contemporary technology, it was found to be more expensive to reuse forms than to produce each of them individually. When next considering the shell of Shenzhen T3, the tower shell of O-14 was turned on its side, and this freedom to customize the shape of each aperture was taken advantage of to enable a wide range of atmospheric and visual effects to be present in the structure without changing the basic form of the vault. Externally the diagrid is entirely regular, allowing for the economy of standardized glazing and cladding units. The cross section of the vault is likewise entirely uniform, allowing for an efficient system of formwork.

Shenzhen T3 also builds on the idea of 'virtual form' first developed in O-14 and attempts to harness it to directly confront the directionless confusion typical of the high-tech airport. By varying the cross-sectional angles of the openings, space and light are modulated to virtually subdivide large, long-span spaces and reinforce circulation routes as the concourse vault appears to change shape while travelers move towards their respective gates. As a result, the spaces of Shenzhen T3 are determined by the orchestration of a linked series of ambient zones created by the continuous modulation of the shell's apertures. In the case of both O-14 and Shenzhen T3, because of the effects of this virtual form, the actual form of the building can be simplified and become subject to logics of production methods, structural analysis, and economy.

Ultimately, any contemporary practice focused on a critical project requires a process composed of both active learning and production. An overall project in architecture is not achieved through case-by-case problem solving, but manifests itself as a continuous trajectory of material and organizational research that continue across many specific design solutions over time. In the case of Reiser + Umemoto, these trajectories of research are then applied to tangible building projects, as in the case of our client-based work, and then, are cultivated and reconfigured in our competition-based work and publications. This way of working is particularly important in order to make sure architectural effects become preeminent in each project, rather than their organization being overly determined by site or program.

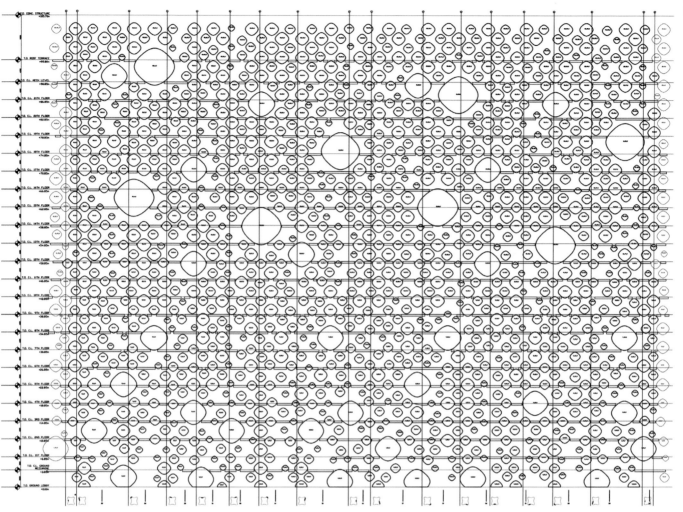

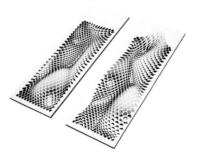

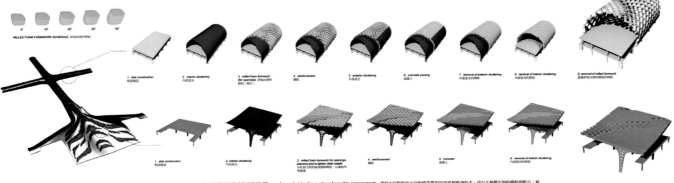

MILLED FOAM FORMWORK SCHEDULE 研泡沫塑料模板

1. slab construction
楼面构造

2. interior shuttering
内部遮光

3. milled foam formwork (for openings)
研泡沫塑料模板 (開孔)

4. reinforcement
鋼筋

5. exterior shuttering
外部遮光

6. concrete pouring
混凝土

7. removal of exterior shuttering
外部遮光的移除

8. removal of interior shuttering
内部遮光的移除

9. removal of milled foam formwork
最後研泡沫塑料模板的移除

1. slab construction
楼面构造

2. interior shuttering
内部遮光

3. milled foam formwork for openings, columns and to lighten shell weight
另孔和立柱的研泡沫塑料模板，以減到外壳重量

4. reinforcement
鋼筋

5. concrete
混凝土

6. removal of interior shuttering
内部遮光的移除

7. removal of milled formwork
研泡沫塑料模板的移除

CONSTRUCTION OF THE TERMINAL AND CONCOURSES WILL UTILIZE CONVENTIONAL CAST-IN-PLACE TECHNOLOGY COUPLED WITH MASS-CUSTOMIZED FORMWORK. The terminal shell is comprised of a lightweight sandwich of slabs between which is a concrete grillage created by void forms. The columns similarly posses hollow cores surrounded by reinforced concrete shells. The concourses will be constructed using slip forming. The variable diagrid can be achieved using a limited number of mass-customized void forms. Mirroring the forms doubles the number of possible arrangements. 登机大厅和机场大厅的建造都将应用常规现浇技术，并与大规模定制的模板相配合。候机楼外壳由轻盈的夹层结构组成，即两层夹板之间的中间是空芯的混凝土格床。类似的是，立柱同样拥有钢化混凝土外壳的空芯结构。登机大厅将使用滑模构造。用一组数量有限的大规模定制空芯结构就能实现可变的斜格网，这些结构呈镜面反射式排列，就会使可能的组合方式成倍增长。

AREA M² 星图区域（平方米）	PEAK POWER GENERATED (KW) 最高发电量（千瓦）	ANNUAL ENERGY SAVED (MWH/YR) 年节能率（年约） 每小时百万瓦时	GHG EMMISIONS AVOIDED (TONNES/YR) 所减温室气体 放量（吨/年）
70,000	9,900	10,400	4,900
52,000	7,425	7,800	3,785
35,000	4,950	5,200	2,456
17,000	2,430	2,560	1,205

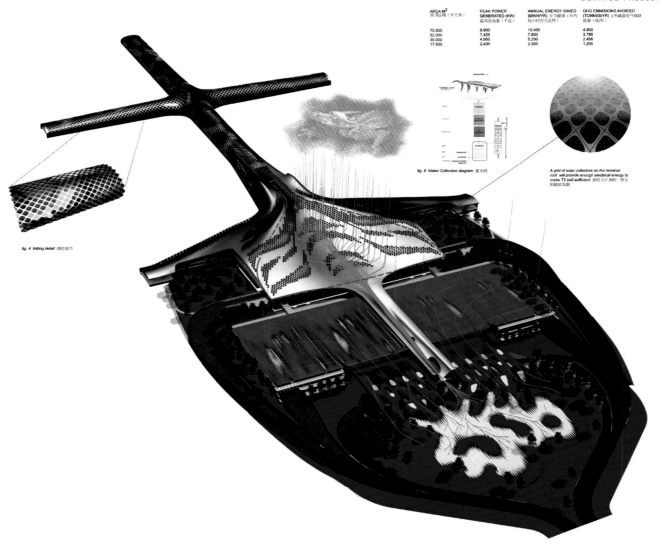

fig. 4 fritting detail 绕结细节

fig. 6 Water Collection diagram 蓄水图

A grid of solar collectors on the terminal roof will provide enough electrical energy to make T3 self-sufficient. 在机大厅顶的一架太 阳缩收集器

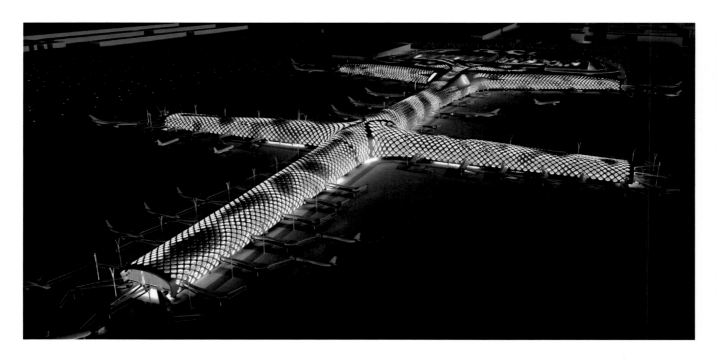

title: **Soundscapes - Smart Ecology**

author: Winka Dubbledam - Archi-tectonics

Soundscapes Archi-Tectonics, NYC

The research in synaesthetic space or the development of soft solids started with the invitation for a group exhibit at the National Building Museum (2003), which included four architects and was curated by Stanley Tigerman. Each architect was asked to build a pavilion, we were asked to build it in AAC [aerated concrete]. Looking at lightweight architecture, we found an interesting connection in sound translated in space. For example the Phillips Pavilion by Le Corbusier in Brussels, [based on the 'hyperbolic parabola' of Iannis Xenakis], the 'bra' installation of Vito Acconci (1990-1991) and the design for the Berlin Philharmony by architect Hans Scharoun (1963) are impressive examples of lightweight architectures reacting to sound.

Soft solid

The phenomenon that sound in itself is an inspiration for architecture, or to an even greater degree, creates architecture-, was proposed as a challenge to re-create and define this installation space. A composer was asked to write a music score for the space, its frequencies were translated in a generative software into surface deformations, thus creating two spatial formulations, the soundscapes. The resulting synaesthetic space is an experience of multiplicities, overlapping sound zones, at once exiting and meditative. The ear will inform the eye and vice versa.......a bodily experience which seduces to relax, stay and dream.

Smart Ecology/ Brussels Park

Ecology (from Greek: οίκος, oikos, "household"; and λόγος, logos, "knowledge") is the scientific study of the distribution and abundance of living organisms and how the distribution and abundance are affected by interactions between the organisms and their environment. The environment of an organism includes both physical properties, which can be described as the sum of local abiotic factors such as insolation (sunlight), climate, and geology, and biotic factors, which are other organisms that share its habitat. The word "ecology" is often used more loosely in such terms as social ecology and deep ecology and in common parlance as a synonym for the natural environment or environmentalism. Likewise "ecologic" or "ecological" is often taken in the sense of environmentally friendly. *(Wikipedia.org)*

Soundscape

The idea of the soundscapes, or "soft solids" was further investigated on an urban level in Brussels; 10 light-weight pavilions and a new park were to be located on a tunnel under Avenue Louise in Brussels. In order to create an equilibrium between the pavilions and the park, we created a music piece. The study of the frequencies distributed over the site, helped integrate the built structures [the Pavilions] with the green zones [the Park], in one fluid movement, where one easily moves in and out of the space.

Smart Ecology

The pavilions, part of the 'green' zone, incorporate both natural green and sustainability. Greenhouses with orchids, bamboo, etc., are incorporated in the pavilions and connect the different zones in the park and create separations between the different areas in the pavilions. Outside in the park, large suspended gardens provide sunshading and rain protection over large squares located at three pivotal points in the park.

FREQUENCY CODING

THE **BASILAR MEMBRANE** IS NARROW AND STIFF AT THE WINDOW END AND WIDE AND FLEXIBLE AT THE APICAL END. THIS **NATURAL TOPOGRAPHICAL DIFFERENCE IN STRUCTURE** RESULTS IN DIFFERENT REGIONS VIBRATING AT DIFFERENT RESONANT FREQUENCIES. THE END NEAR THE STAPES (WINDOW END) VIBRATES AT HIGH FREQUENCIES WHEREAS THE APICAL END VIBRATES AT LOW FREQUENCIES. INFORMATION ABOUT THE VIBRATION AT DIFFERENT LOCATIONS ALONG THE BASILAR MEMBRANE IS RELAYED TO THE AUDITORY CORTEX BY THE NERVES SYNAPSING WITH THE HAIR CELLS AT THOSE LOCATIONS. **THE AUDITORY CORTEX IS THEREFORE SAID TO BE TONOTOPICALLY MAPPED**, I.E. THE BASILAR MEMBRANE IS REPRESENTED POINT FOR POINT ON THE AUDITORY CORTEX.

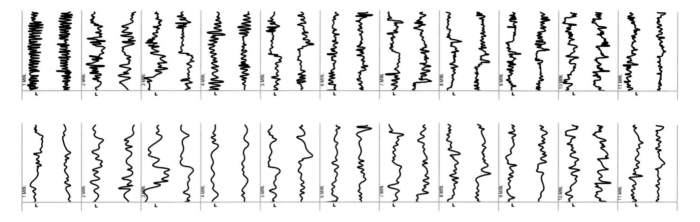

AUDIO FREQUENCY MATRIX CONVERSION/SECTIONAL STUDIES **: 0-11MIN. DURATION FOR MOVEMENT T1/T2/T3.**

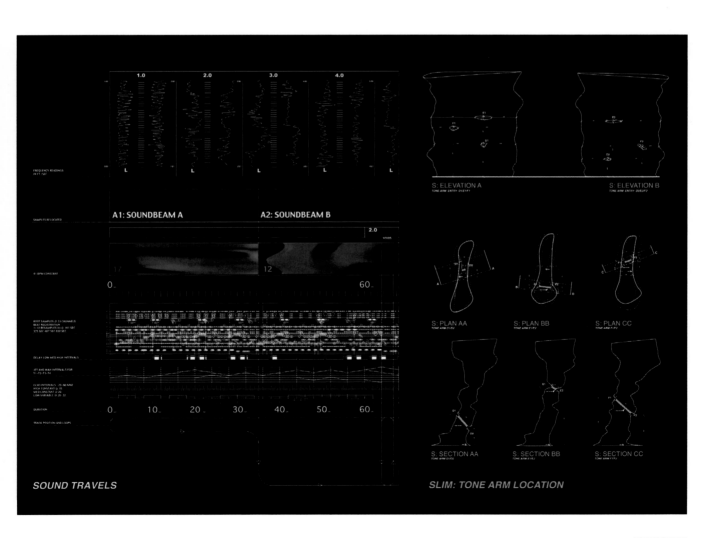

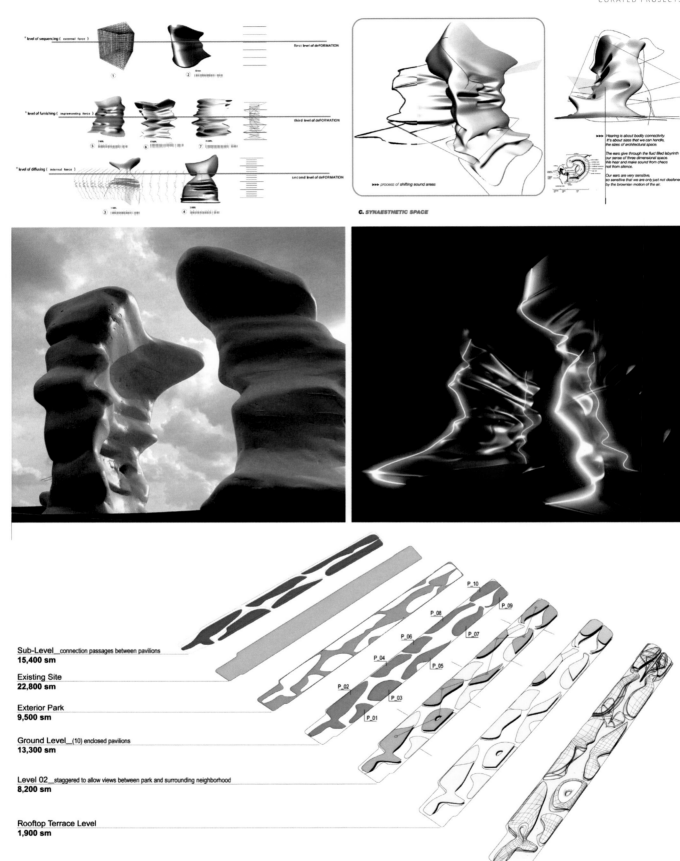

* level of sequencing (external force)

first level of deFORMATION

* level of furnishing (implementing force)

third level of deFORMATION

* level of diffusing (internal force)

second level of deFORMATION

>>> process of shifting sound areas

C. SYNAESTHETIC SPACE

>>> Hearing is about bodily connectivity.
It's about sizes that we can handle,
the sizes of architectural space.

The ears give through the fluid filled labyrinth -
our sense of three dimensional space.
We hear and make sound from chaos
not from silence.

Our ears are very sensitive,
so sensitive that we are only just not deafened
by the brownian motion of the air.

Sub-Level_connection passages between pavilions
15,400 sm

Existing Site
22,800 sm

Exterior Park
9,500 sm

Ground Level_(10) enclosed pavilions
13,300 sm

Level 02_staggered to allow views between park and surrounding neighborhood
8,200 sm

Rooftop Terrace Level
1,900 sm

Total Enclosed Pavilion
38,800 sm

P_10

P_08

P_09

P_06

P_07

P_04

P_05

P_02

P_03

P_01

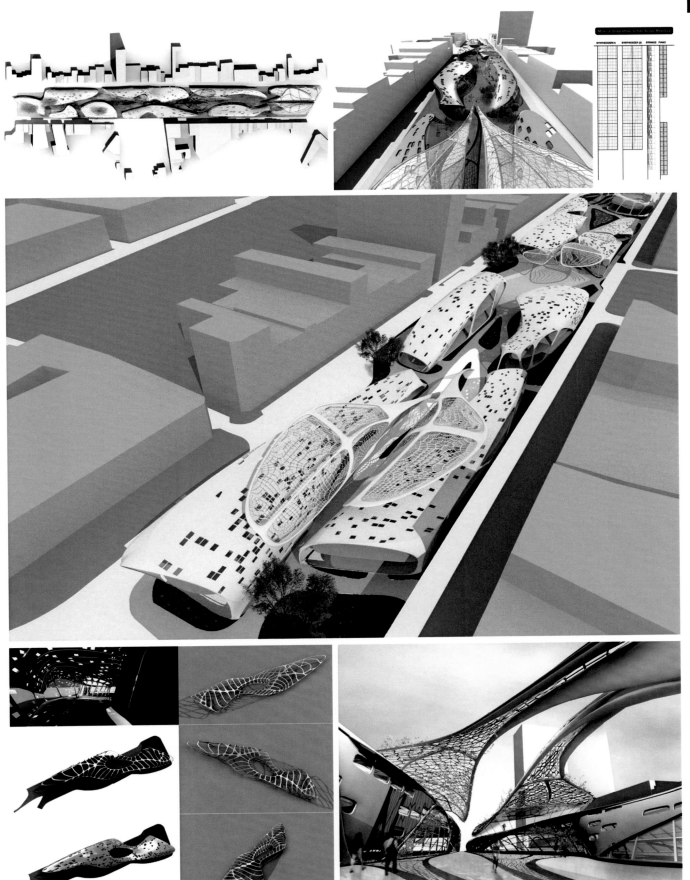

title: **Design Evolution of Tower Structure - Case of Phare Tower**

author: Thom Mayne, Satoru Sugihara - Morphosis

1) Introduction of Diagrid

In the original design in the competition phase, the shape of Phare tower was formed mainly by limitation of the site for foundation structure and wind load in the air and those compound constraints generated the irregular shape and various unique edge conditions. Diagrid structure was introduced as an integration system to deal with those various structural conditions and to serve as a design layer to emphasize continuity and consistency over the irregularity of the form of the tower.

2) Maximization of Continuity

However, we initially experienced difficulty to model consistent and continuous diagrid geometry on the highly irregular boundary shape with the existing modeling platforms. After the competition phase, we developed in-house custom software for the design of diagrid. The function of software is a type of polygon mesh relaxation implementing simulation of physical forces like tension treating each node of diagrid as an agent and letting them negotiate with neighboring nodes to relocate itself to an optimized location. With this software, continuous and consistent diagrid geometry on the whole tower could be modeled.

3) Maximization of Rationality

As the result of maximization of continuity, the irregularity in the boundary condition was all distributed into every member of diagrid geometry ending up making structural members all unique. To produce rational geometry, within some areas having similar members, identical members are copied to maximize the repetition. However this process inevitably enhances the difference and discontinuity between the rational areas. These differences can be absorbed in buffering areas between rational areas by the mesh relaxation algorithm maximizing continuity and smoothness of tangency. Because the algorithm is designed to deal with irregular boundary conditions, this process to increase repetition areas means refining the boundary for the algorithm by excluding the repetition areas. In this way, continuity and consistency are maintained in the maximization process of rationality.

4) Minimization of Cost

When the project was struggling to reduce its cost, the feedback from structural engineers brought an opportunity of huge cost reduction by treating the diagrid as columns and bracings. Due to the code, two diagonally intersecting members in diagrid are both required to have certain, fairly large dimension as a primary structural member but if one of diagonals is vertical enough to be seen as a column which is still primary structure, another diagonal can be seen as a bracing which can be secondary structure only for lateral load and its dimension can be radically smaller than another. Following this logic the whole diagrid geometries were remodeled to have vertical members.

At this moment, another constraint came from the view point of interior space design to maximize the efficiency of use of office space. To match the location of vertical columns with the grid of interior space partitions, vertical columns were relocated. After maximizing the vertical geometries, matching them with the grid, and mediating the difference between separately modified areas by the mesh relaxation algorithm, the structure engineer analyzed structural load distribution to remove excessive lateral support at the upper part of the tower and the structure geometries were finalized.

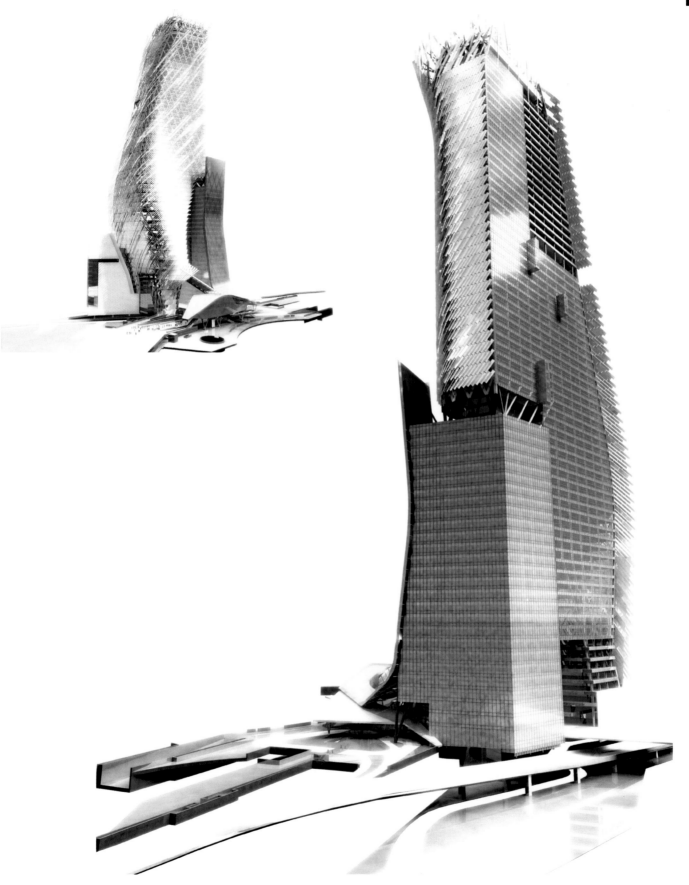

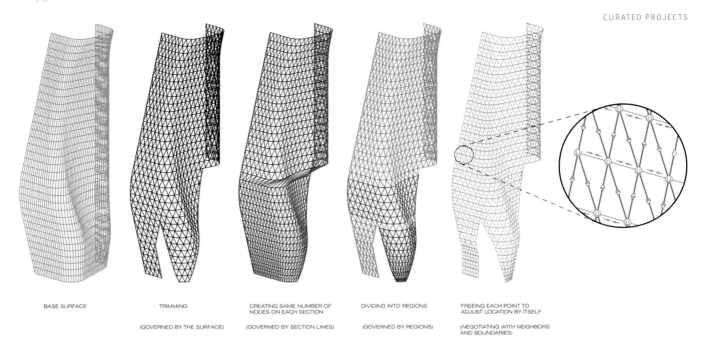

BASE SURFACE

TRIMMING

(GOVERNED BY THE SURFACE)

CREATING SAME NUMBER OF
NODES ON EACH SECTION

(GOVERNED BY SECTION LINES)

DIVIDING INTO REGIONS

(GOVERNED BY REGIONS)

FREEING EACH POINT TO
ADJUST LOCATION BY ITSELF

(NEGOTIATING WITH NEIGHBORS
AND BOUNDARIES)

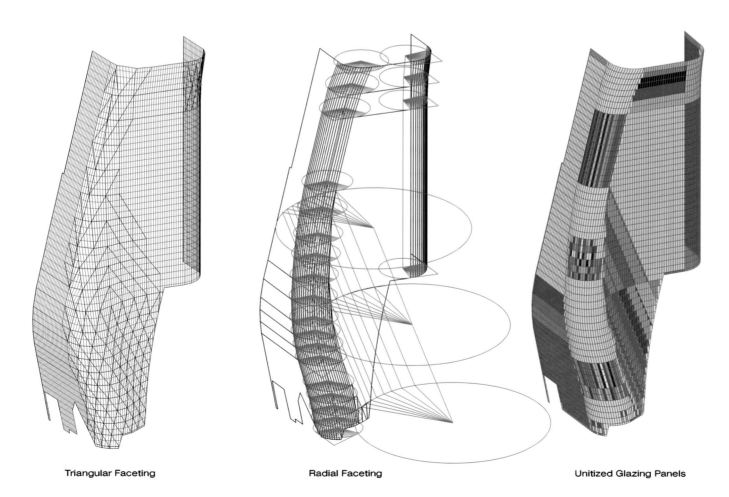

Triangular Faceting

Radial Faceting

Unitized Glazing Panels

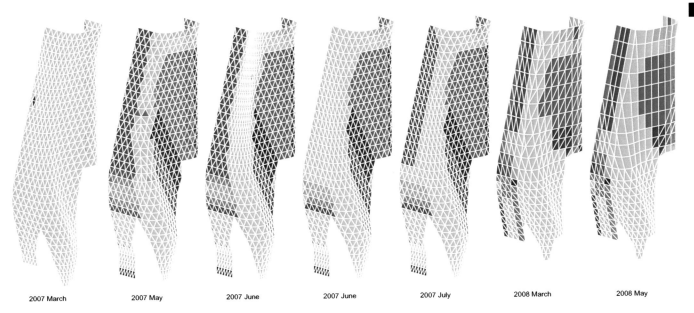

| 2007 March | 2007 May | 2007 June | 2007 June | 2007 July | 2008 March | 2008 May |

EVOLUTION OF STRUCTURE

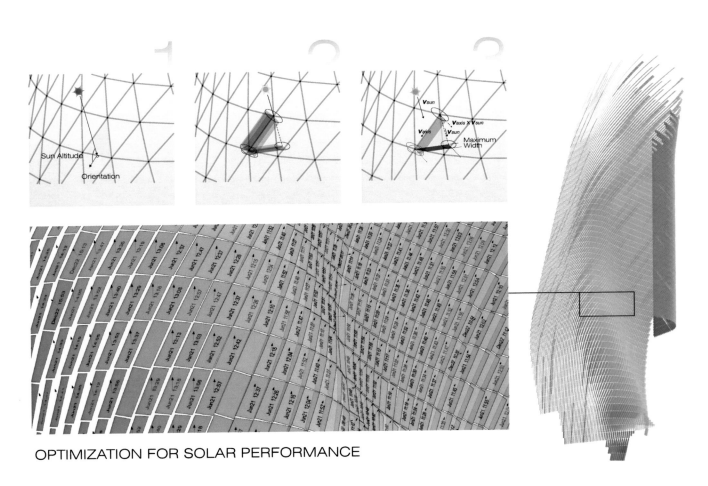

OPTIMIZATION FOR SOLAR PERFORMANCE

739 panels	42 panels	28 panels	19 panels	12 panels	12 panels	4 panels	4 panels	2 panels	2 panels	2 panels	2 panels	2 panels	2 panels	2 panels	2 panels
501 panels	41 panels	28 panels	18 panels	12 panels	12 panels	4 panels	4 panels	2 panels	2 panels	2 panels	2 panels	2 panels	2 panels	2 panels	2 panels
387 panels	40 panels	28 panels	17 panels	12 panels	11 panels	4 panels	4 panels	2 panels	2 panels	2 panels	2 panels	2 panels	2 panels	2 panels	1007 unique panels
364 panels	35 panels	26 panels	17 panels	12 panels	10 panels	4 panels	4 panels	2 panels	2 panels	2 panels	2 panels	2 panels	2 panels	2 panels	total 5100 panels
339 panels	33 panels	25 panels	17 panels	12 panels	9 panels	4 panels	4 panels	2 panels	2 panels	2 panels	2 panels	2 panels	2 panels	2 panels	
73 panels	32 panels	22 panels	15 panels	12 panels	9 panels	4 panels	3 panels	2 panels	2 panels	2 panels	2 panels	2 panels	2 panels	2 panels	
69 panels	31 panels	22 panels	13 panels	12 panels	9 panels	4 panels	3 panels	2 panels	2 panels	2 panels	2 panels	2 panels	2 panels	2 panels	
57 panels	31 panels	21 panels	13 panels	12 panels	8 panels	4 panels	3 panels	2 panels	2 panels	2 panels	2 panels	2 panels	2 panels	2 panels	
55 panels	30 panels	21 panels	13 panels	12 panels	8 panels	4 panels	3 panels	2 panels	2 panels	2 panels	2 panels	2 panels	2 panels	2 panels	
51 panels	30 panels	20 panels	12 panels	12 panels	7 panels	4 panels	3 panels	2 panels	2 panels	2 panels	2 panels	2 panels	2 panels	2 panels	
47 panels	30 panels	19 panels	12 panels	12 panels	4 panels	4 panels	2 panels	2 panels	2 panels	2 panels	2 panels	2 panels	2 panels	2 panels	
45 panels	28 panels	19 panels	12 panels	12 panels	4 panels	4 panels	2 panels	2 panels	2 panels	2 panels	2 panels	2 panels	2 panels	2 panels	

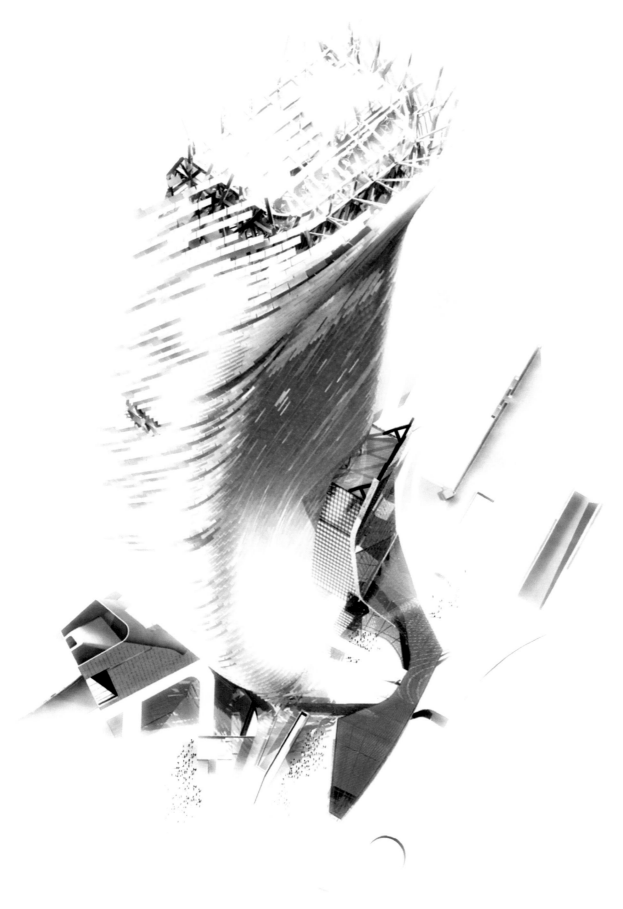

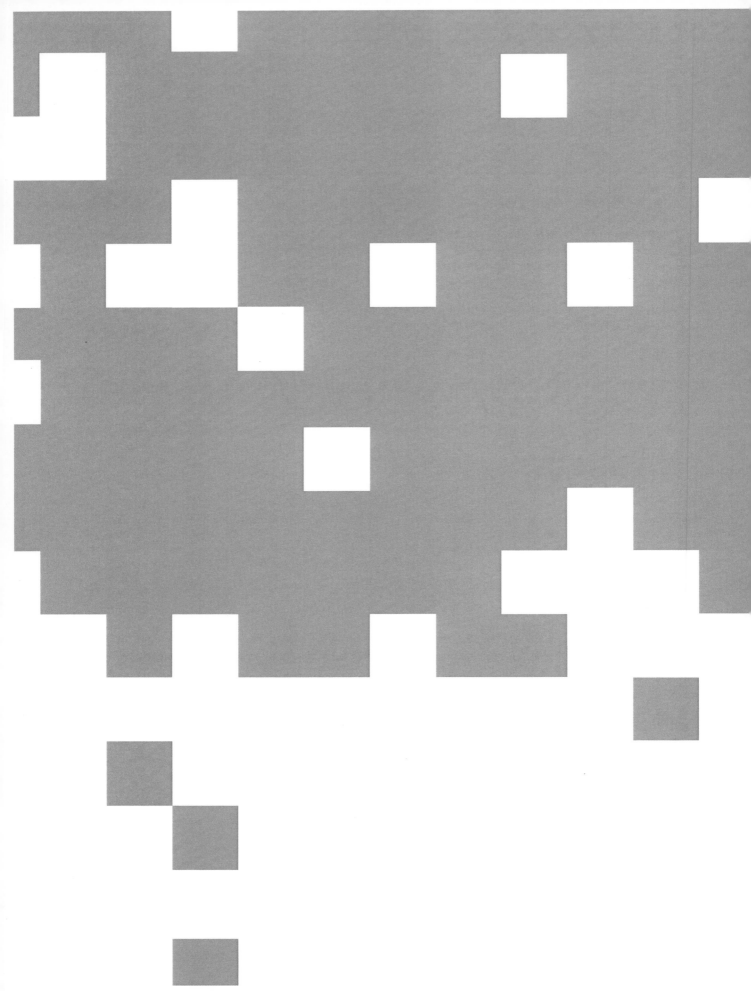

Peer Reviewed Projects
The Great Hall Gallery of The Cooper Union

Listener
A probe into information based material specification

Mette Ramsgard Thomsen - *CITA Centre for IT and Architecture, Royal Danish Academy of Fine Arts, School of Architecture, Denmark* Ayelet Karmon - *Department of Interior Building and Environment Design, Shenkar College of Engineering and Design, Israel* Eyal Shaeffer - *Textile Design Department, Shenkar College of Engineering and Design, Israel*

Digital fabrication has introduced a new material nearness in architectural practice. Material understanding in traditional architecture relies on diagrammatic notations that are interpreted by the builder-craftsman. As designers engage with unprecedented levels of material control and complexity, the design of material behaviour becomes part of the architectural remit. This leads to a new understanding of materials as variegated and responsive to the particular design criteria of their implementation.

To fully exploit these advances it is important to develop models by which variegated material designs can become part of architectural practice. The design project Listener was developed as an interdisciplinary collaboration between textile design and architecture, exploring how information based fabrication technologies are challenging the material practices of architecture. The two fold information based strategies present in Listener are first, the development of direct interfaces between parametric design and textile fabrication. Second, by integrating structural and actuated materials, the project presents the making of a new class of materials that are computationally defined as well as controlled.

Developing the Listener prototype
Listener is a robotic membrane defined by a design scenario that determines its performance and design criteria. As an architectural membrane it is listening to its environment and reacting to its change by intermittently inflating and deflating.

Interfacing material thinking directly with production
Listener is developed across a diagrid base pattern. Using Grasshopper as a platform for parametric design, we developed means of deforming the base pattern through local deformations. A scripted interface was developed to the CNC Stoll knitting machine, bypassing its design software and writing directly in machine code. Using the Visual Basic interface in Grasshopper we used the point location as developed in the diagrid to define a base structure for material specification. Each individual knitting needle and yarn carrier is addressed directly through the VB definition. In this way we were able to control the design of the surface creating a graded material that is continually changing in its structural composition.

Considering materials as active
Listener is composed of four different fiber types. Two different conductive yarns were used to enable interaction. On the backside, an insulated wire was used as a capacity sensor. The change in capacitance is used as an input to a micro computer triggering a high pressure valve system, making the surface inflate and deflate. A second pattern of conductive fibers are knitted into the front of the material. These paths line the air chambers at either edge. As the chambers expand and contract, they make the conductive paths touch, acting as a soft switch, effectuating secondary movement cycles that propagate through the material as self actuated waves.

Conclusion
As a speculative project, Listener asks how highly-specified materials can be conceived and by which technologies we can imagine their production. In the development of Listener, we have created information based materials joining architecturally designed environments with CNC textile fabrication. We have explored textiles as a model for conceiving and testing this new emergent practice.

Credits
The project relies on cross disciplinary collaborations with: Ami Cang, the Knitting Lab, the Textile Design Department, Shenkar College of Engineering and Design. Tzach Harari, Robotics Lab, Yair Reshef, Interactive, the Department of Interior Building and Environment Design. Shimrit Cohen, student. Conductive yarn contributor: Silverell (Shieldex)

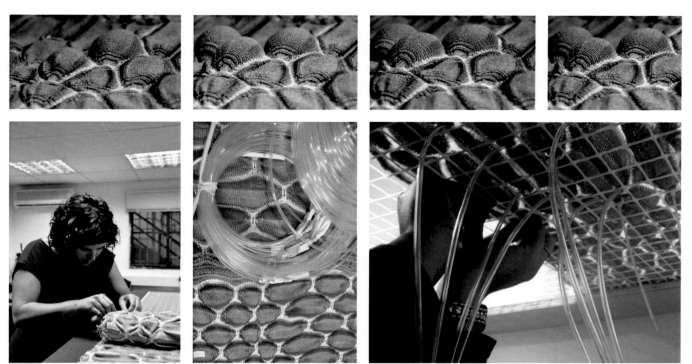

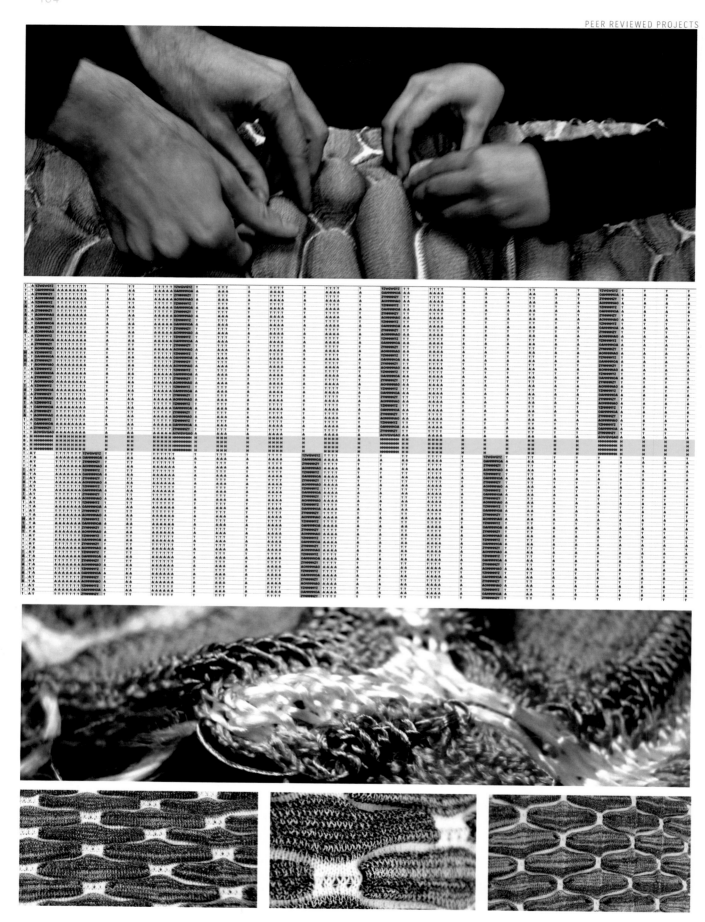

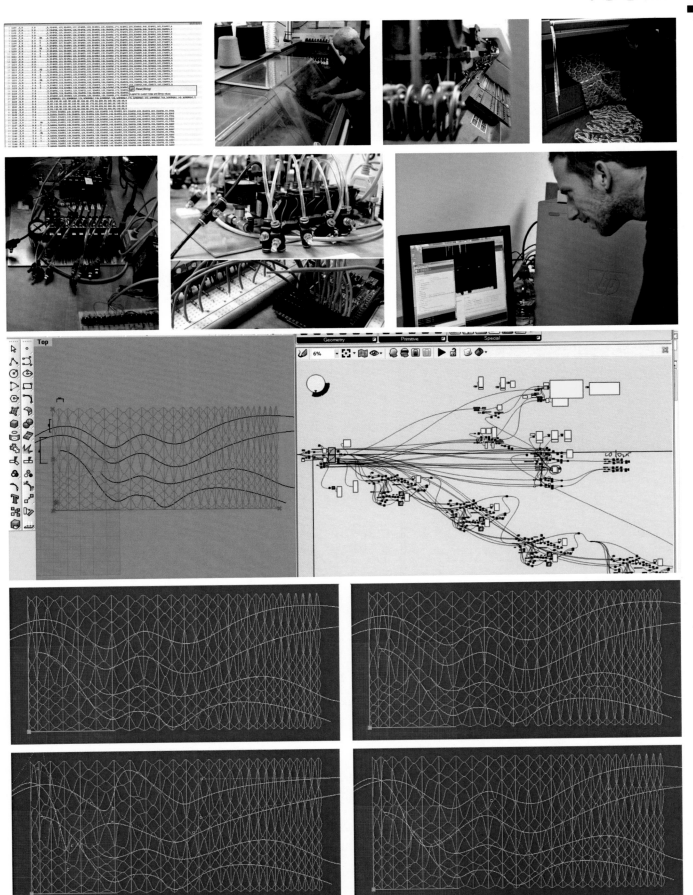

Scentisizer
Scent engine and tangible interface for composing and performing scentscapes

Rodolphe el-Khoury - *Khoury Levit Fong, University of Toronto, Canada*
Nashid Nabian - *Arsh Design Studio, University of Toronto, Canada*

Scentisizer allows for the orchestration and delivery of complex fragrances by giving precise control over the constitution and diffusion of scent accords in dynamic compositions. A tangible interface combines haptic and graphic features for managing an array of sixty-four scent dispensers that maps a wide-ranging olfactory field. Users can manipulate individual scent containers, much like organ stops, to compose and time an accord in a direct and intuitive fashion. They can also control them with greater complexity and precision by means of a digital graphic user interface that allows for multi-channeled sequencing and modulation of scent tones and dynamics. The analogue controls provide the haptic means for tangibly sculpting and visualizing olfactory phenomena while the digital features add functionality and web connectivity, allowing Scentisizer to perform digitized olfactory scores stored locally or accessed wirelessly.

Haptic User Interface: Scent Topography
In the perfume industry, an architectural/topgraphgic metaphor has traditionally served to disentangle the intricately imbricated constituents of multi-faceted fragrance, re-arranging them in three distinct strata: top notes, middle notes, and base notes.

Scentisizer adopts this schema for the haptic interface to facilitate the intuitive understanding and building of complex olfactory phenomena. Users can control the behavior of their scent-compositions over a prescribed period--programmed via an integrated touch-pad, by shaping the array of dispensers into the desired pyramidal form--a tangible rendition of the topographic metaphor. The slightest elevation from the default low position activates a dispenser while varying elevations trigger different pr- programmed diffusion cycles:

from 0 to 2 inches up: the dispenser produces a base note

from 2 to 4 inches up: the dispenser produces a middle note

from 4 to 6 inches up: the dispenser produces a top note

Higher positions within each range translate into greater intensity at the peak of the programmed cycle.

Once the cycle is launched, the motorized tubes are automatically animated, sinking gradually into their default rest position while transcoding the status of the the unfolding olfactory phenomenon at any given time into a topographic image, a tangible and instantly graspable 3-d diagram of the evolving scent structure.

Graphic User Interface: Multi-Track Composition and Performance
The graphic user interface enables greater control over the scent-dispensing array, providing user-adjustable parameters for shaping the dynamics of the individual constituents of the fragrance and the overall effect over time.

In "Compose" mode, users define the general parameters of the phenomenon such as overall intensity and duration. They can also call up each individual scent from a grid of colored dots representing the array to view and graphically plot its evolution in the 'multi-track' composition.

The course of individual scents is plotted by means of a graph with a nerb-controlled curve that users can adjust with great precision. The curve graphically maps the way each scent is launched, sustained and decayed. The graphs of all active scents are visible behind the one that is called up for adjustment so as to facilitate composition of individual 'tracks' in relation to others and with an understanding of the whole.

In "Perform" mode, users can monitor the evolution of the fragrance in a graphic animation that visualizes the varying states of its constituent parts in a grid of expanding or shirking dots.

Scent Mapping

The scents assigned to each dispenser are mapped according to a variation on the Fragrance Wheel, a taxonomy developed by the fragrance industry for a user-friendly classification of scents in distinct but related families: Floral, Fresh, Oriental, Woody, and Aromatic Fougère. These categories are arrayed in color-coded gradients, with fixative scents bridging between different families such as Musk and Coumarin occupying the center of the field.

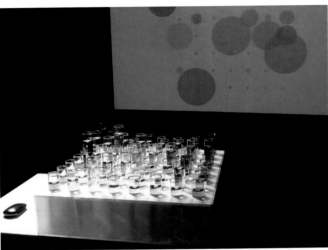

Duration of Performance > 01:44:15
Repeat > OFF

You are composing the "Thyme" note now!

shrink · expand Perform reset

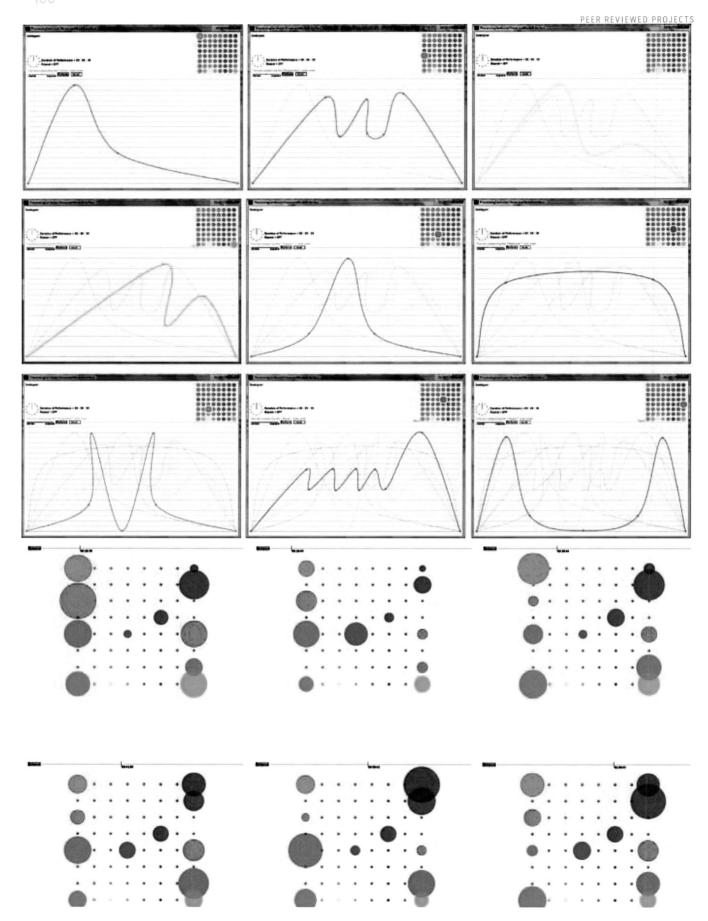

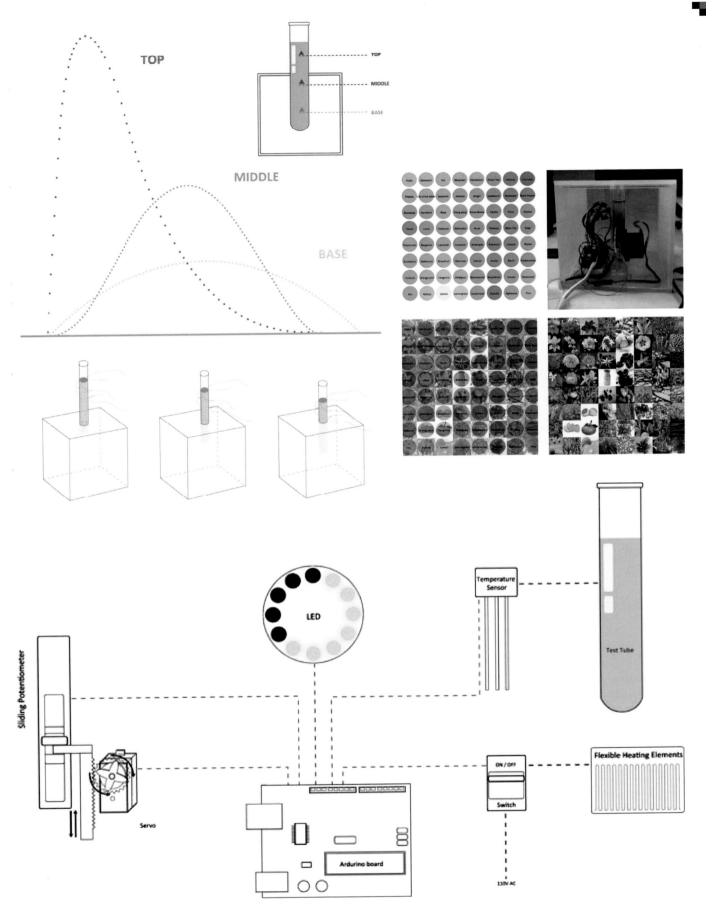

XeromaxSensing Envelope
Nervous systems, responsive skins

Jason Kelly Johnson - *Future Cities Lab / California College of the Arts, United States*
Nataly Gattegno - *Future Cities Lab / California College of the Arts / UC Berkeley, United States*

Around us is a protective wall of senses that gets denser and denser. Outward from the body, the senses of touch, smell, hearing and sight enfold man like four envelopes of an increasingly sheer garment.
-Jacob von Uexküll, An Introduction to Umwelt

The xeromax sensing envelope is an ongoing research project being developed by a multi-disciplinary group of experimental architects, engineers, programmers, and interaction designers. Each contributor is fundamentally concerned with the latent terrain at the intersection of the physical and digital worlds. The specific theme of ACADIA 2010 [LIFE in:formation] is of particular interest to our group and is closely related to both the conceptual and technical aspects of this project.Our installation is a responsive prototype for an architectural surface that can sense, plan, and actuate based on inputs from its physical environment, its parametric 3D model, and the internet. The suspended prototype encourages interaction and playfully responds through light and shape changing skins.

There are several layers to the prototype pictured in this document: [a] The host surface is constructed of hundreds of folded, perforated hexagonal synthetic units; [b] The interactive LED/Sensor units; [c] The robotic hexagonal blossoms; [d] The wires connecting the surface to the ceiling mounted micro-controllers.

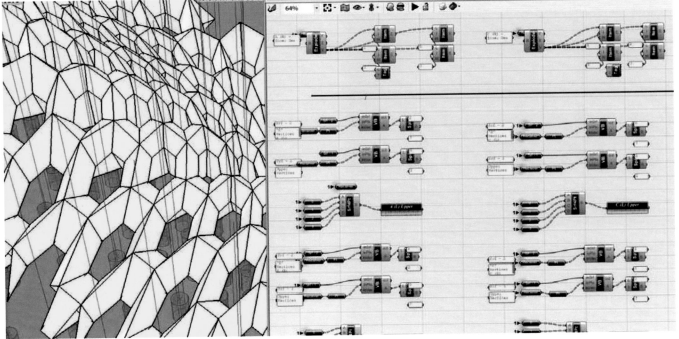

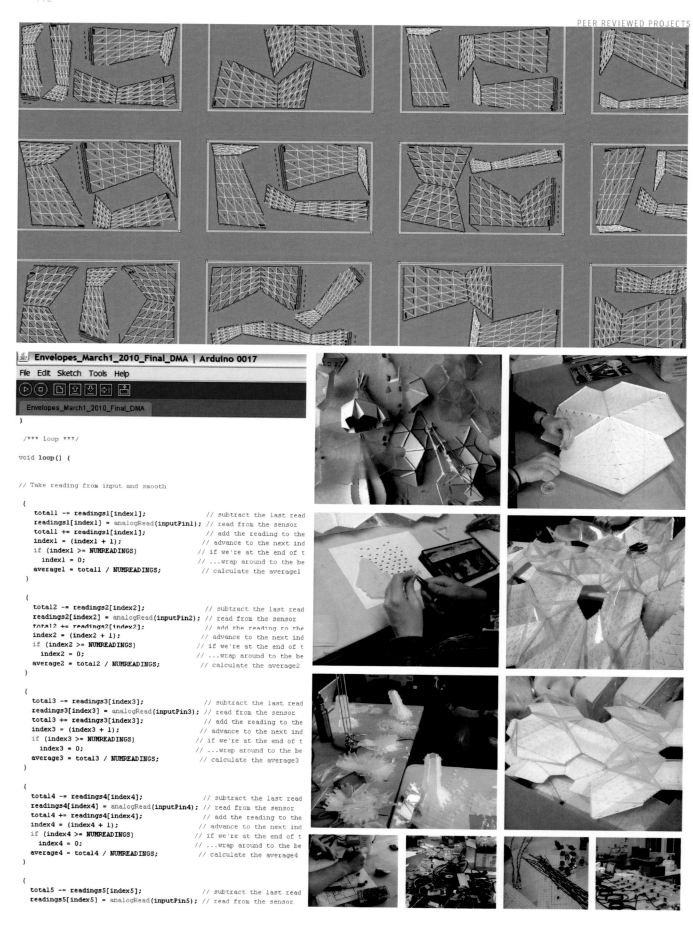

Envelopes_March1_2010_Final_DMA | Arduino 0017

File Edit Sketch Tools Help

Envelopes_March1_2010_Final_DMA

```
}

/*** Loop ***/

void loop() {

// Take reading from input and smooth

 {
    total1 -= readings1[index1];              // subtract the last read
    readings1[index1] = analogRead(inputPin1); // read from the sensor
    total1 += readings1[index1];              // add the reading to the
    index1 = (index1 + 1);                    // advance to the next ind
    if (index1 >= NUMREADINGS)                // if we're at the end of t
      index1 = 0;                             // ...wrap around to the be
    average1 = total1 / NUMREADINGS;          // calculate the average1
 }


 {
    total2 -= readings2[index2];              // subtract the last read
    readings2[index2] = analogRead(inputPin2); // read from the sensor
    total2 += readings2[index2];              // add the reading to the
    index2 = (index2 + 1);                    // advance to the next ind
    if (index2 >= NUMREADINGS)                // if we're at the end of t
      index2 = 0;                             // ...wrap around to the be
    average2 = total2 / NUMREADINGS;          // calculate the average2
 }


 {
    total3 -= readings3[index3];              // subtract the last read
    readings3[index3] = analogRead(inputPin3); // read from the sensor
    total3 += readings3[index3];              // add the reading to the
    index3 = (index3 + 1);                    // advance to the next ind
    if (index3 >= NUMREADINGS)                // if we're at the end of t
      index3 = 0;                             // ...wrap around to the be
    average3 = total3 / NUMREADINGS;          // calculate the average3
 }


 {
    total4 -= readings4[index4];              // subtract the last read
    readings4[index4] = analogRead(inputPin4); // read from the sensor
    total4 += readings4[index4];              // add the reading to the
    index4 = (index4 + 1);                    // advance to the next ind
    if (index4 >= NUMREADINGS)                // if we're at the end of t
      index4 = 0;                             // ...wrap around to the be
    average4 = total4 / NUMREADINGS;          // calculate the average4
 }


 {
    total5 -= readings5[index5];              // subtract the last read
    readings5[index5] = analogRead(inputPin5); // read from the sensor
```

Morpholuminescence

Joshua Vermillion, Mahesh Senagala, Elizabeth Boone, Eric Brockmeyer, Adam Buente, Kyle Perry - *Ball State University, United States*

A student-led studio project, MorphoLuminescence utilizes an understanding of fashion photography to find its form and provide optimized lighting, enhancing the experience of trying on clothing. A three-point lighting set up is commonly used by fashion photographers, arranging a bright key light above eye level, in combination with softer fill and back lighting to create subtle shadows and a three dimensional effect.

Comprised of custom laser-cut "petals," "stems," and hinges, Morpholuminescence was pre-assembled for testing prior to shipping in pieces to site. MorphoLuminescence provides variably tuned hue and light intensity levels in order to affect the fitting room experience and adapts its form to accommodate changes in the space. In its idle state, the dimly lit surface of petals hangs free, signaling to consumers that it is ready for use. Through simple infrared sensors, human presence and variations in the space are analyzed, initiating its state of change. Differences in height are read by the sensors and interpreted by two Arduino microprocessors, which drive servo-motors, in order to actuate the surface. MorphoLuminescence amplifies the experience of the individual by expanding and contracting, recognizing when a user is bending over or reaching up to remove clothing, only arriving at its state of pose when the consumer is ready. In this final state, each panel of the surface is backlit with an individual light source. Relative to the ratios of the three-point lighting set up, more illumination occurs where the density of panels increases. MorphoLuminescence focuses on efficient, optimized lighting for the individual, as well as physically amplifying the experience of change in a fitting room.

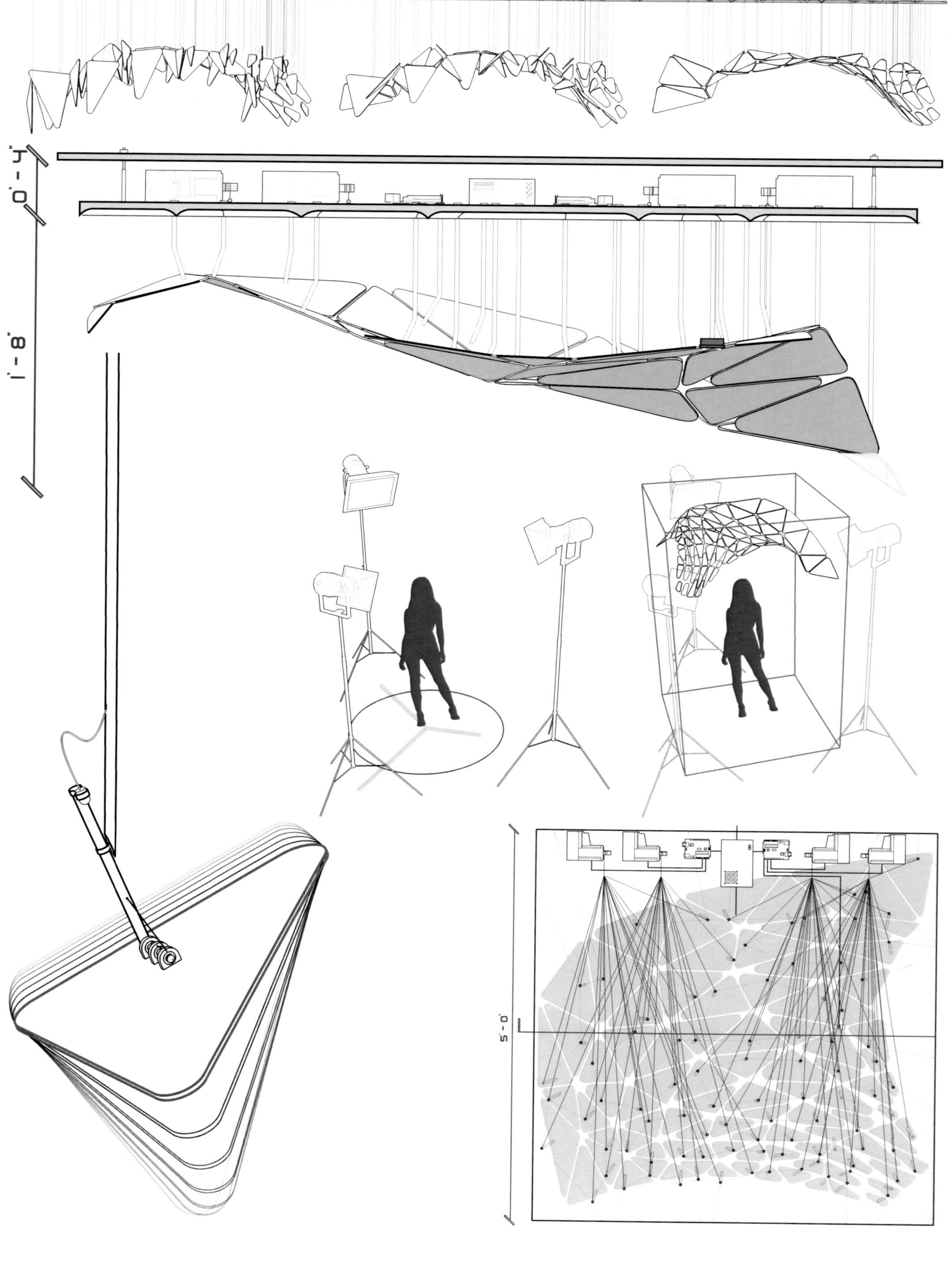
0' - 4"
1' - 8"
5' - 0"

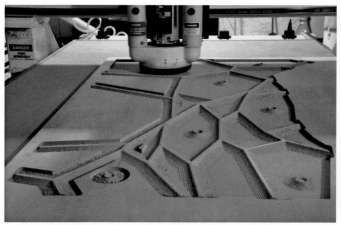

Voxel

Arshia Mahmoodi, Reza Baherzadeh - *II-I, United States*

This project has attempted to address a basic negotiation between an interpreted media from photonic motion to the literal capability of an envelope to intercede as a medium, while providing the architecture for the synchronous light emitting elements. This capability has manifested itself in our project by superseding the traditional role of the architecture of interactive facades, which have remained neutral in their mediatory role, with a 3-dimensional composition that interacts directly and provides systems architecture for the interactive system.

The project takes advantage of the overlayment of several speeds:
1- Motion graphics produced by the interactive LED elements.
2- Motion produced by the 3D array of interactive LED elements.
3- Motion produced by the vibrissal elements relative to the light elements.
4- Motion produced by the moiré effect of the structural fins.
5- Motion produced by lines of flow (initial crystallization of the project).

Located at the epicenter of the legendary Sunset Strip, the project has aimed to engage the public in ways that a traditional architecture could fend off. Rather than proposing walls as a territorial tactic for defining private boundaries, the project, through the implication of a vibrissal semi-transparent envelope, invites the gaze through the building to create a quality of mediative milieu, which at the same time erodes the continuum of building facades along the Sunset Strip.

This project, since its initiation in 2004, has attempted to break the tradition of the decade old electronic facade typology that ordinarily utilizes the pixilated lights as solid surface material. A deliberate attempt to blend the inherent dynamics of controlled lighting modules with physical potentials of a fluid structure has managed to render the project unique to its space-time.

The project is made of approximately 1200 tubular elements, each of which include an LED module (pixel) at its tip. It sets off to explore the dynamics of kinetic architecture through non-movement, by taking advantage of scale and flow relative to the mobile observer. The overlapping of such dynamics, with the appearance of motion graphics, creates virtually infinite modes of emergence. The vibrissae—much like the 'pin impression toy'—are capable of manual retraction in order to change the appearance of the facade over time. Having left open the potential of interactive capabilities of that technology, the project aims to be an urban canvas for motion graphic art, creating installations that are interactive to the response of the environment or the audience (i.e. movement of pedestrians, ambient sound response, vehicular interactivity, etc). It also hopes to serve as a ceremonial piazza for the City of West Hollywood 's public inaugural events.

The project was fabricated entirely from a digital output and assembled onsite. The gill system was lasercut locally from a digital file; the tubular elements were cut to size from generic aluminum tubing; and the light emitting modules were custom fabricated in China from a digital mockup.

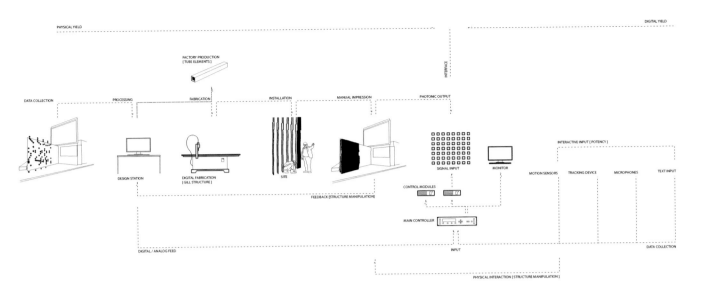

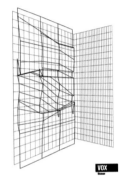

VOX

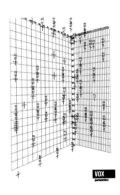

VOX

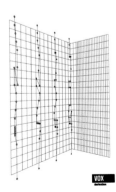

VOX

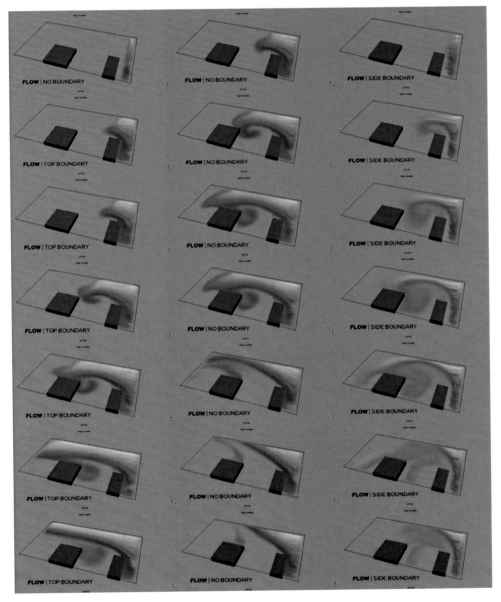

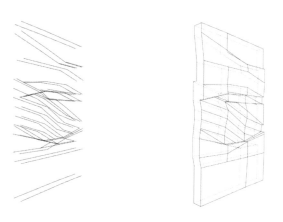

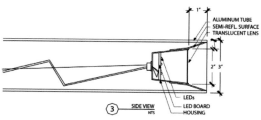
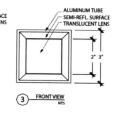

1″

ALUMINUM TUBE
SEMI-REFL. SURFACE
TRANSLUCENT LENS

2″ 3″

LEDs
LED BOARD
HOUSING

③ SIDE VIEW
NTS

ALUMINUM TUBE
SEMI-REFL. SURFACE
TRANSLUCENT LENS

2″ 3″

③ FRONT VIEW
NTS

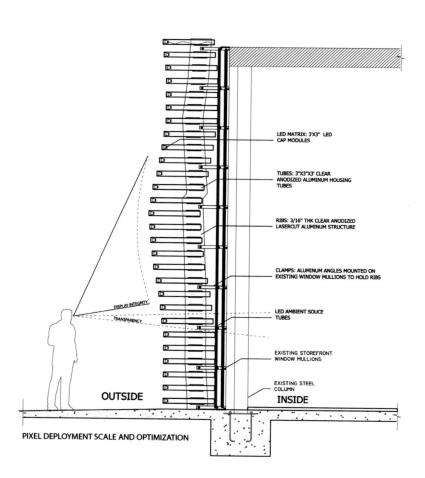

LED MATRIX: 3"X3" LED
CAP MODULES

TUBES: 3"X3"X3' CLEAR
ANODIZED ALUMINUM HOUSING
TUBES

RIBS: 3/16" THK CLEAR ANODIZED
LASERCUT ALUMINUM STRUCTURE

CLAMPS: ALUMINUM ANGLES MOUNTED ON
EXISTING WINDOW MULLIONS TO HOLD RIBS

LED AMBIENT SOUCE
TUBES

EXISTING STOREFRONT
WINDOW MULLIONS

EXISTING STEEL
COLUMN

DISPLAY INTEGRITY

TRANSPARENCY

OUTSIDE

INSIDE

PIXEL DEPLOYMENT SCALE AND OPTIMIZATION

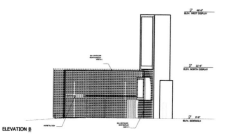

SITEPLAN

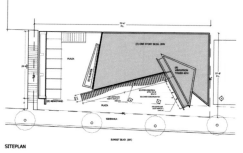

ELEVATION B

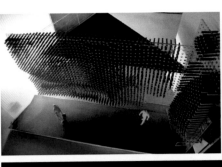

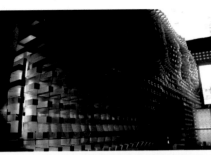

Behavior, Not Intelligence

Rob Ley - *Southern California Institute of Architecture, United States*

In the last century, the potential of an interactive, information based architecture has shown itself to offshoot in many varied directions. The most immediate is often seen and understood as a scenario where the individual is served by his surroundings. All of these proposals rely on a degree of intelligence of the machine. Essentially, the environment must be designed smart enough to either predict, or at least understand in real time, the needs and wishes of the user such that an immediate technological gratification will soon follow.

Five years ago, our studio began a line of research directed by the assumption that the responsibility of architecture can and should be more than to provide shelter. More specifically, it would seem that as fields outside of architecture (transportation, medicine, communication, etc.) have evolved exponentially as they directly emanate from technological developments, architecture will also benefit from advances in material science, computational capacities, and information fluidity. Rather than continue in the belief that good, contemporary architecture is that which serves, our work over the last several years has focused on creating architecture that contributes a behavioral position. That is to say, an environment that serves the user is less beneficial than one that exhibits a degree of willfulness and offers the user companionship.

Our first line of research looked at the role that robotic toys have played in people's lives. Adults, as well as children, have a capacity to respond emotionally to animated entities, not based on the perceived intelligence of the creature, rather in response to its motion and behaviors. If a small robotic dog appears to be plastic and driven by motors and gears, it doesn't matter. What matters is the manner in which it moves and how it seemingly responds to the owner. The capacity for humans to project affection onto artificial life forms has shifted our focus within our behavioral research of environmental interaction. Thus behavior, a term we use as a description of how and why something moves has become a pinnacle concept in the work of the past 5 years. What we find interesting is that behavior may ultimately be more important than intelligence as we strive for a viable model of interactivity of space and the user.

A recent completed project that pulls from this research was comprised of hundreds of responsive surfaces, powered by NiTinol, a shapememory alloy wire. This spatial arrangement, combined with an interface fed by an RGB camera and processed with software written for the Max/MSP platform, created an environment that responded to inhabitants. The processing of responses was guided by varying criteria ranging from simple location and proximity, to more judgmental decisions such as the color of clothing and whether users were alone or in groups. More interesting than the arbitrary processing criteria was the responses from the users once they realized that their presence and actions had an immediate affect on the space. Rather than focusing on the reasons for responsiveness, people were attracted to the nature of the motion, quite similar to that seen in the relationship of robotic pets and their owners. This consistent response by the varying users has clarified earlier observations that intelligence and the capacity to process information may be overrated criteria within a study of interactive environments and artificial intelligence. Instead, behavioral qualities, particularly kinematic motion and indirect 'responsiveness' are more successful in creating a connection between inhabitants and their environment. Continuing research projects are now looking at the role that scale and materiality have within this proposition.

Fig. 1: Aluminum tabs organize flow and orientation of fins and create an interface for dynamic control system

Fig 2: Animated sequence diagram demonstrates fin motion as it ripples through gallery space

5

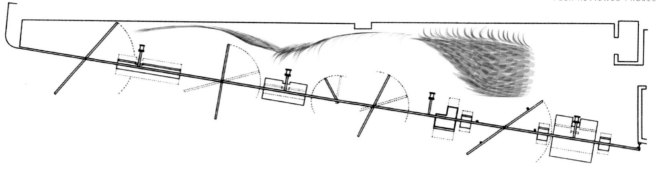

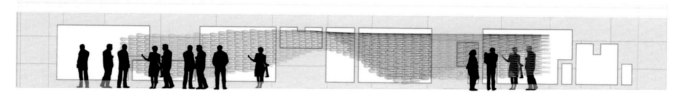

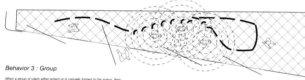

Behavior 3 : Group

When a group of users either enters or is casually formed in the space, their presence will cause both a noticeably heightened degree of motion (fin curvature) and velocity (speed of motion). The group effect attempts to create a dynamic, somewhat tepentatial from the individual behavior, and in turn, tries to create a new relationship between the user(s) and the responsive space.

Interactive Behaviors

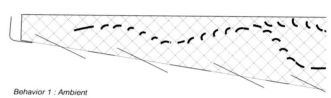

Behavior 1 : Ambient

When the immediate space is unoccupied for a period of time greater than 5 minutes, Reef exhibits an ambient behavior. In this mode, the fins are actuated in a random fashion similar to a "white noise" pattern. This mode is essential in the relationship between space and user as it establishes the architecture's autonomy when a user first enters the room. If the space were to remain motionless until a user were to enter, the perception would be that the space is 'awakening' to serve. Instead the user, by entering the space, is interrupting a condition already underway.

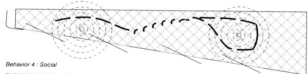

Behavior 4 : Social

This final behavior is transitionary. It attempts to encourage separate individual users to form a group while in the space. In previous behaviors, the immediate responsiveness of the space is directly tied to a user's location and distance to the fins. In this mode, however, the clusters of fins closest to the individual users remains static. Instead, clusters of fins in an area between the two users becomes active, as a way to motivate each user to come together towards the motion.

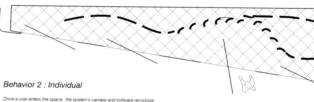

Behavior 2 : Individual

Once a user enters the space, the system's camera and software recognize that someone is now present and Ambient mode segways into Individual mode. At this time, the user's location is mapped and their proximity to the Reef is used as an input into the system. As long as the user remains alone, the space will respond directly to their proximity and walking speed in a direct and linear fashion.

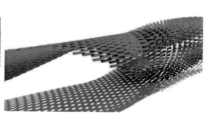

Fig 7: Interior view showing the layering of aluminum framework and translucent fins

Fig 8: Responsive system recognizes and processes the location of the user and detects if they are alone or in a group. Varying behaviors exhibited through the motion of the fins are then triggered based on defined criteria.

Fig 9, 10: Interior view showing the layering of aluminum framework and translucent fins

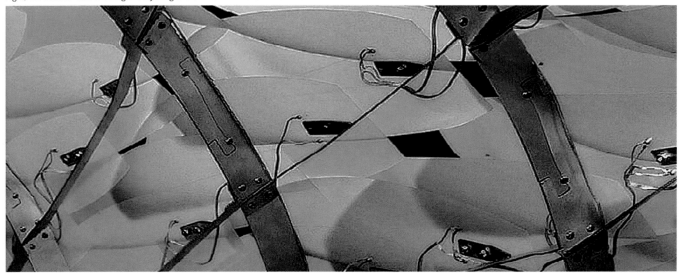

Heterogeneity
Math driven form seeking + fabrication

Ming Tang - *Assistant Professor, University of Cincinnati, United States*
Jonathon Anderson - *University of North Carolina Greensboro, United States*

Heterogeneity focuses on the study of mathematics as an embedded genotype of spatial arrangement within procedural modeling. The influence of digital media and information technology on architectural education and practice is increasingly evident. Digital technology has reconditioned the design process by establishing new processes and techniques of fabrication. This reconditioning has influenced how we operate as architects.

Heterogeneity proposes an interdisciplinary research where computational 3D forms are digitally fabricated in order to explore the demand for high performance and spatial interaction within the architectural field. This is accomplished through the exploration of several form finding/fabrication techniques. The results are novel artifacts that manipulate the physical landscape.

In this research, the designers explored the manipulation of a planar surface through algorithmic equations. The use of mathematics to drive form generated unlimited possible artifacts that were bounded only by the parameters that the designers input. The adaption of several variables was used to control the repetition and resolution of these artifacts through an exhaustive combination of values. This additive information evolved independently in order to yield a more fabrication friendly form. The fabrication of physical prototypes was explored through Fused Deposition Modeling (FDM), CNC milling, and laser cutting. Digital fabrication was used as a means to inspire designers to use unconventional mathematical forms in architectural design, which was traditionally restrained by difficulties in translating the digital design and visualization to the physical landscape. The manifestation of the digital and physical world is becoming a seamless transition through the transferring of numerical code.

A project titled Mathmorph used animated 2D graphics to produce a sequence of profiles that were used to construct a 3D model through a control variable of time which acted as the 4th dimension. The results of this exploration were porous structures that interlock/intertwine and allowed for natural ventilation and indirect lighting. The designers viewed these artifacts as a potential building component—similar to CMUs—that focused on the potential transformative spatial layout.

A series of abstract building masses were designed with the focus on their potential transformative spatial layouts. This generation of an abstract mathematic form using equations was studied to manifest interlocking volumes of solid and void spaces. We adapted several variables to control the repetition and resolution of these interlocking spaces. From a large number of outcomes, only several ideal spatial arrangement solutions were selected by reviews and then used as the genotype for the next operation.

The use of these mathematically driven forms could generate porous buildings masses that were non-site-specific and allow for maximum heat gain/loss and natural wind-flow. The math form was considered as a solid mass and sliced into a multi-story skyscraper. By interlocking two forms the generation of natural program issues solved themselves. Offering a laminated weave of two structures, one residential tower and one vertical farm, resulted in various combinations of artificial space and natural space that united each level in a cohesive and coherent landscape.

The designers created a high degree of complexity and explored the dynamic possibilities of spatial arrangement with relatively simple input information. The computational approach to design allowed for two areas of interest in the architectural field to combine digital form finding and digital fabrication. The complexity was easily fabricated by components built into the parametric model that produced the file documentation needed to realize the artifact in the physical landscape. In this process, the mathematic model demonstrated an unlimited potential of form exploration from sets of parameters. The reviewers selected the desired control parameters to manipulate the form and generated spatial organization, which ultimately proved that a parametric model can be optimized by a fabrication limitation.

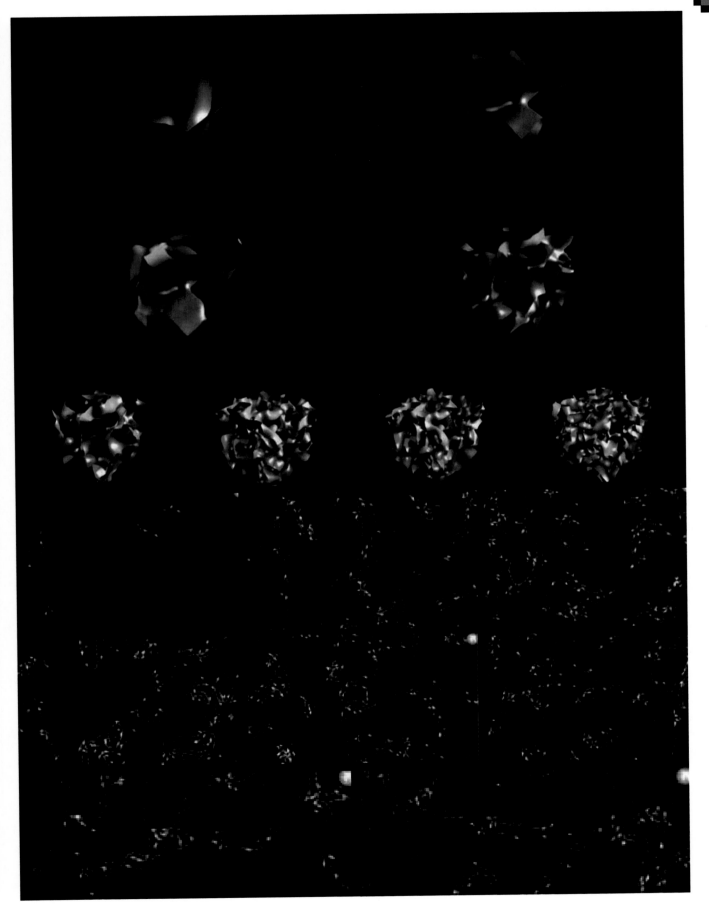

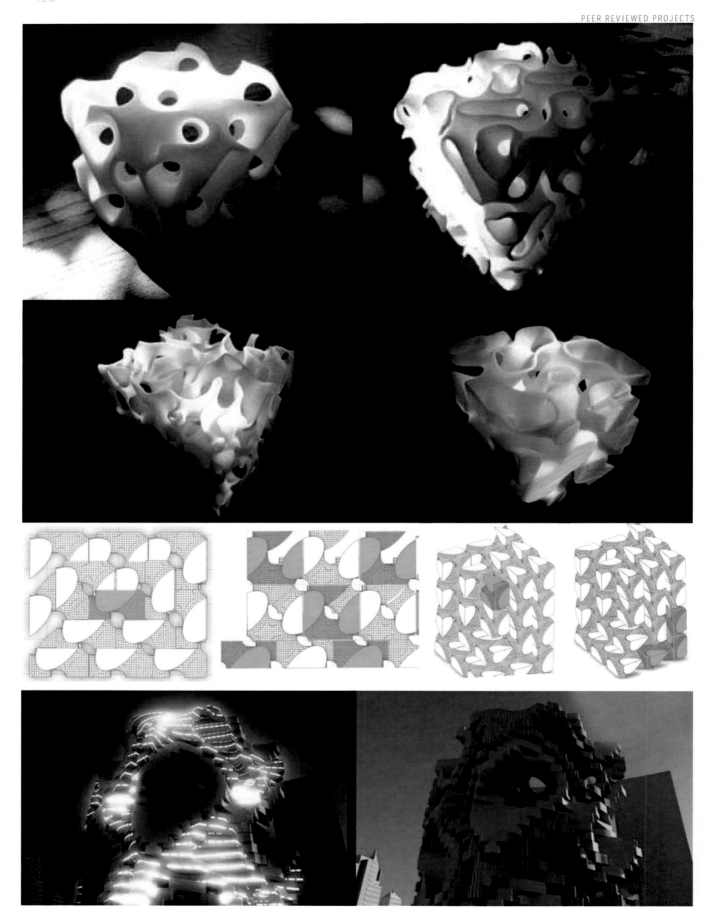

Fibre Composite Adaptive Systems

Maria Mingallon - *ARUP & Architectural Association, Canada*
Sakthivel Ramaswamy, Konstantinos Karatzas - *Architectural Association, United Kingdom*

The premise of this research is to emulate self-organisation processes in nature by developing a fibre composite material system that could sense, actuate and hence efficiently adapt to changing environmental conditions. Fibre composites which are anisotropic and heterogeneous offer the possibility for local variations in their material properties. Embedded fibre optics would be used to sense multiple parameters and Shape memory alloys integrated in a fibre composite material for actuation. The definition of the geometry, both locally and globally would complement the adaptive functions and hence the system would display 'Integrated Functionality'.

'Thigmo-morphogenesis' refers to the changes in shape, structure and material properties of biological organisms that are produced in response to transient changes in environmental conditions. This property can be observed in the movement of sunflowers, bone structure and sea urchins. These are all growth movements or slow adaptations to changes in specific conditions that occur due to the nature of the material: fibre composite tissue. Nature has limited material; remarkably all of them are fibres, cellulose in plants, collagen in animals, chitin in insects and silk in spiders. Natural organisms have advanced sensing devices and actuation strategies which are coherent morpho-mechanical systems with the ability to respond to environmental stimulus.

Architectural structures endeavour to be complex organisations exhibiting highly performative capabilities. They aspire to dynamically adapt to efficient configurations by responding to multiple factors such as the user, functional requirements and the environmental conditions. Existing architectural smart systems are aggregated actuating components assembled and externally controlled, whose process of change is essentially different from that of thigmo-morphogenesis. In a leaf, the veins account for its form, structural strength and nourishment, nevertheless they are an integral part of the sensing and the actuation function. This process of a coherent self-autonomous multi-functionality could be termed as 'Integrated functionality'. Emulating such a Morpho-mechanical system with sensors, actuators, computational and control firmware embedded in a fibre composite skin was the core of the research presented herein.

Performative abilities and intelligence of the fibre composite adaptive system proposed, springs from the integrated logics of its material behaviour, fibre organisation, topology definition and the overall morpho-mechanical strategy. The basic composite consists of glass fibres and a polymer matrix. The sensing function is carried out through embedded fibre optics which can simultaneously sense multiple parameters such as strain, temperature and humidity. These parameters are sensed and processed as inputs through artificial neural networks. The environmental and user inputs, inform the topology to dynamically adapt to one of the most efficient configurations of the 'multiple states of equilibrium' it could render. The topology is defined as a multi-layered tessellation forming a continuous surface which could have differentiated structural characteristics, porosity, density, illumination, self-shading and so on. The actuation is carried out through shape memory alloy strips which could alter their shape by rearranging their micro-molecular organisation between their austenitic and martensitic states. The shape memory alloy strip is bi-stable, but a strategic proliferation of these strips through a rational geometry could render several permutation and combinations creating multiple states of equilibrium, thus enabling continuous dynamic adaptation of the structure.

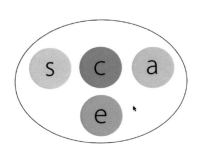

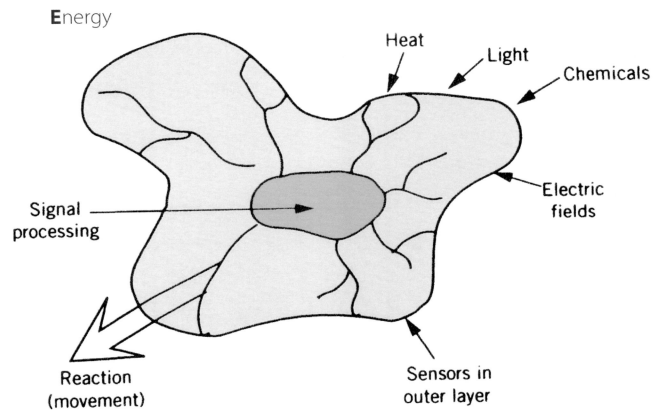

Sensing
Actuation
Control
Energy

Heat

Light

Chemicals

Signal
processing

Electric
fields

Reaction
(movement)

Sensors in
outer layer

Material
Structural Fibres

Sensing
Fibre Optic

Actuation
Shape Memory Alloy

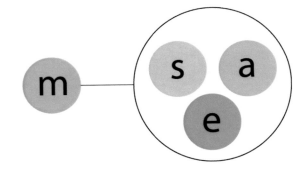

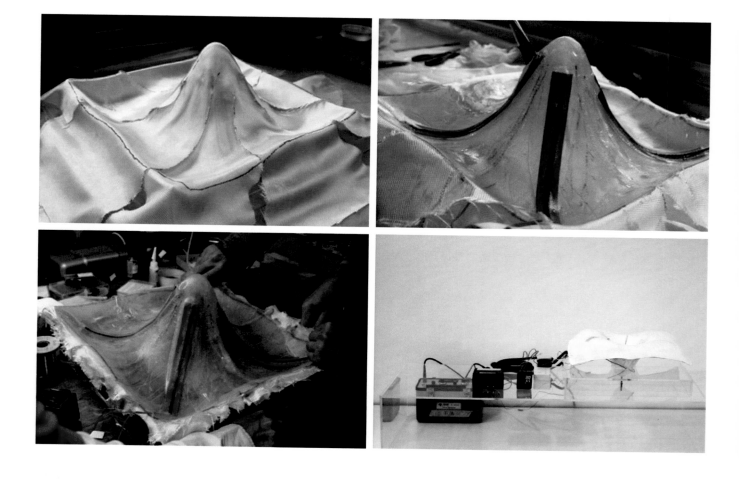

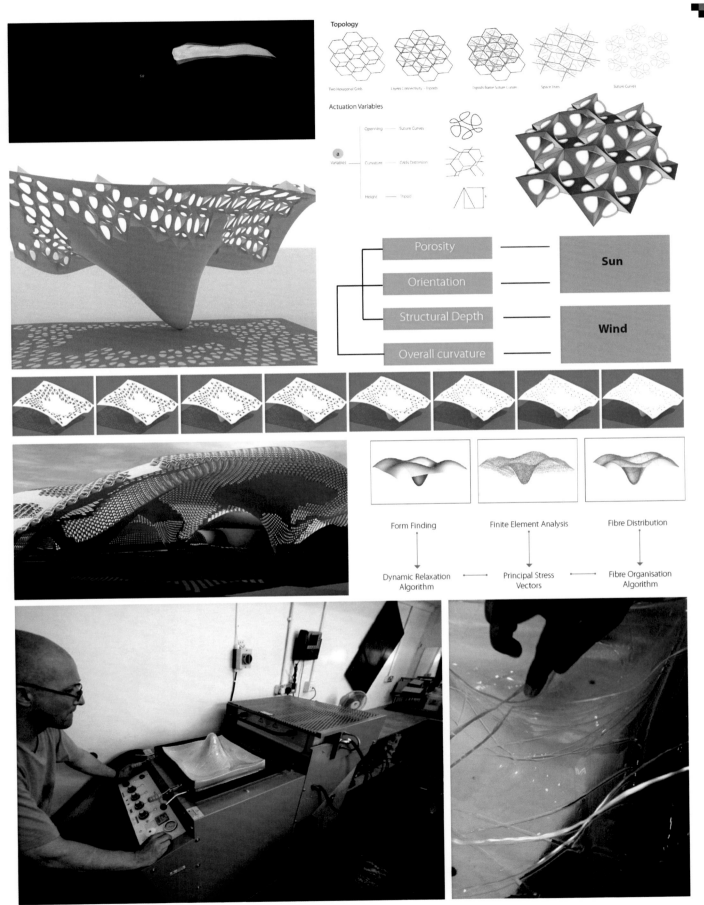

Topology

Two Hexagonal Grids — Layers Connectivity - Tripods — Tripods frame Suture Curves — Space Truss — Suture Curves

Actuation Variables

a
Variables

Openning — Suture Curves

Curvature — Grids Distorsion

Height — Tripod

Porosity	Sun
Orientation	
Structural Depth	Wind
Overall curvature	

Form Finding — Finite Element Analysis — Fibre Distribution

Dynamic Relaxation Algorithm ← → Principal Stress Vectors ← → Fibre Organisation Algorithm

Procedural Pipeline: The HWYLtL Exhibit

Robert Trempe - *Temple University, United States*

Introduction

The "HWYLtL" project began as a vector-based graphical articulation manifest from user sensory "wishes" supplied by an architectural client building a new home. It was crafted to help the designer in understanding the needs of the client and potential behaviorally-based design strategies through emergent, patterned, non 1:1 results. Executed via the use of a procedural network with parametric inputs supplied by the client (submitted as a simple multi-week, multi-answer survey tied directly to inputs within the procedural network), a vector-based graphical "depiction" of the user's hopes, dreams, and senses towards the occupation of domestic space was generated.

"HWYLtL" seeks to exploit the design "pipeline" from the beginning of process via technical advances in procedural modeling tied to visual acuity and interpolation, proposing connections from concept to execution. The first step (the mapping of quantitative data) serves as instruction our "output" for every other aspect in the design "pipeline." This output has countless potential, operating as "Rorschach Test" for the changes in client sensory perception and attitude towards space over time, as a graphical "instigator" for the designer (using the formal results to unlock emergent design potential), and even as instructions for CNC production by using the resultant vector patterns as paths for mills and laser/plasma cutters in the building of parts for the house.

Mechanical and Technical: The Mapping Process

In this somewhat "Rube Goldberg-sek" procedural model, data drove the generation of three-dimensional information with the procedural network transforming this information into two-dimensional results, all done live and on the fly (via the connection established in Grasshopper). Each week's results could be immediately linked to the model, with each week's results affecting a singular instance of the model. As new results were obtained, a new iteration was superimposed on the previous weeks result, building a time-based composite of the client's decisions. As these mappings were to be read in a somewhat analytical fashion, the removal of perspective-based information was paramount if one was to be able to understand relational changes throughout the model.

Conceptual and Concrete Power

As a "concrete tool of construction," the basic procedural network is augmented and added to as a method for moving from conceptual design to that of design fabrication. The "lines" of the resultant mappings can easily be manipulated and converted (via additions to the procedural network) to tool-paths for use by CNC routers, plasma and laser cutters, each helping in the production of architectural elements for the resultant house. Procedural "filtering" can also be added to the existing network to help in shaping the results to operate more in a three-dimensional manner, aiding in the fabrication of elements such as wall panels, windows, and other architectural systems now being driven by automated construction methods. By utilizing the procedural network and linking data via a design pipeline through to construction, the "tool" used in articulating ideas and spatial visualization becomes the same "tool" used in construction, thereby embedding data and virtual craft into the physical construction in ways that complete the pipeline.

Summary

In the end, the "HWYLtL" project is able to display methods by which designers can use procedural networks as organizers and articulators of a "process pipeline." Procedural modeling should not be seen as an end-all-be-all tool for the design of architecture, nor does this paper demonstrate that a singular network can simply "design any architecture." In fact this paper demonstrates quite the opposite as the initial rules that governed the design of a specific type of architecture were encoded into the network early on in the design process. Specificity (critical to any design) in approach and flexibility (tools that allow the designer to consistently engage his/her critical eye in the design process) are still paramount in this process as they should be in any design process. The approach demonstrated here is meant to display how new techniques can enhance the rigor we use in a design process, and how the results of that rigor (from the marking of the "tool" to the data being articulated) can be better reflected through output.

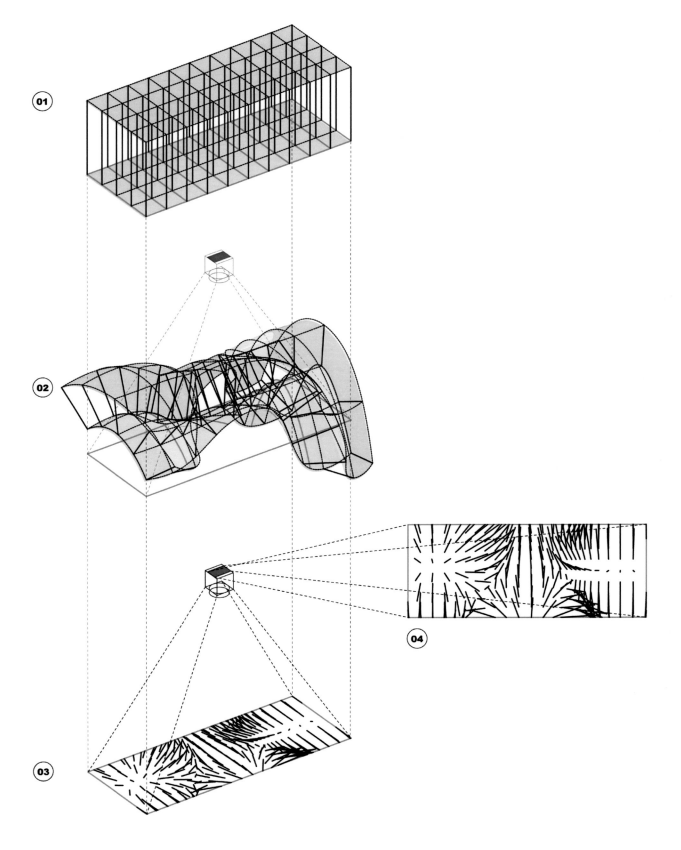

01

02

03

04

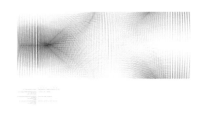

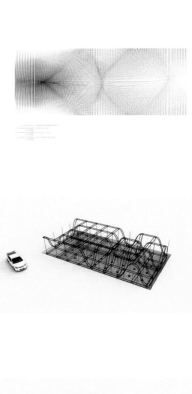

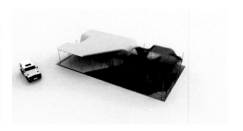

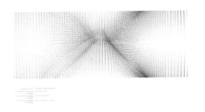
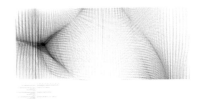

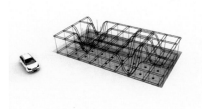

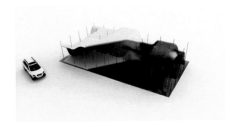

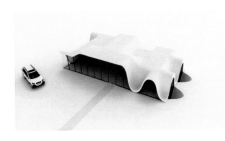

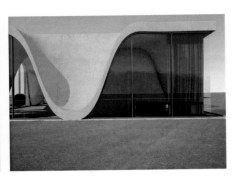

Lux Nova/Kaleidoscape

The history of architecture is laced with moments of invention that reinforce the link between material practices, social practice, and the narrative of environments.

Lonn Combs, Rona Easton - *Easton+Combs, United States*

The history of architecture is laced with moments of simple invention that reinforce the link between material practices, social practice, and the narrative of environments. In addressing the question of an environmental structure for the MoMA PS1 courtyard, we were inspired by the story of an old material and it's reinvention that profoundly affected the connection between social narrative and the environment.

In twelfth century Paris, the Abbey Saint Denis experienced a substantial reconstruction that included, for the first time, the use of polychromatic dyed glass to extend the narrative possibilities of painting into the surface of the apse window. Upon completion, Abbot Suger was so moved by the multicolored cast of light and it's narrative power that he declared it the 'Lux Nova' or the 'new light.' This was to become a primary architectural practice incorporated in the collective experience of the gothic period and beyond.

Although the PS1's environmental structure may have less sacred aspirations for the employ of innovative material techniques, the collective narrative of the 'Warm-Up' ritual and more contemplative museum installation narrative offer unique cultural counterpoints for the exploration of architectural invention.

The architectural installation is primarily an environmental structure that proposes a diaphanous multihued surface that spans above and thickens locally to provide multiple scales of habitation, both collective and intimate. The structure produces both temperate environments and luminous atmospheres that drift dynamically with daylight. This narrates a landscape of light, color, and ambient environments that create temporary atmospheres for contemplative and collective occupation.

The proposal explores the basic environmental and cultural performance of extruded cellular polycarbonate. Polycarbonate is a featherweight, high strength building material which is sustainably manufactured and 100 percent recyclable. The architectural use of the polycarbonate leverages both the high strength and ultralight weight as a series of blades in an interwoven lattice structural skin. The geometric organization of the structure creates a fenestrated surface that produces a moiré visual field condition.

With this innovation, the narrative power of the material's properties is revealed and attention is returned to a basic condition of architecture as an influencer of local atmospheres through material means.

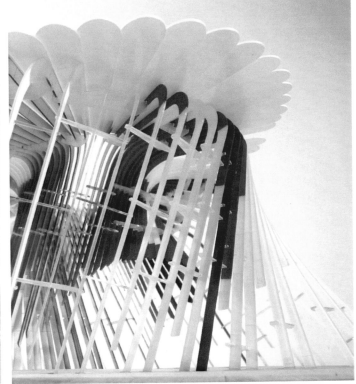

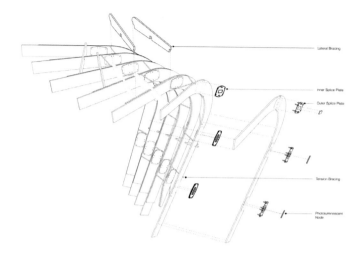

Assembly Diagram

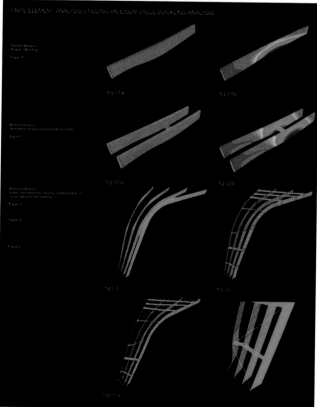

FINITE ELEMENT ANALYSIS UTILIZING AN EIGEN VALUE BUCKLING ANALYSIS

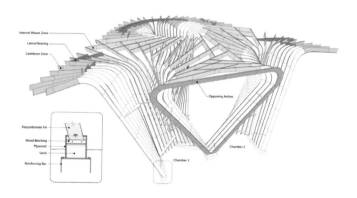

	Polycarbonate	Glass	Steel	Aluminum	Wood	Bamboo	Concrete
PCF	75	160	490	165	40	40	150
Equivalent Weight	1	5	10	4	2.5	2.5	15

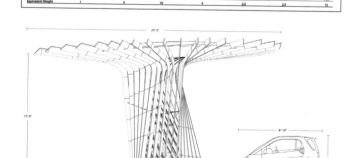

1,487 lbs   1,600 lbs

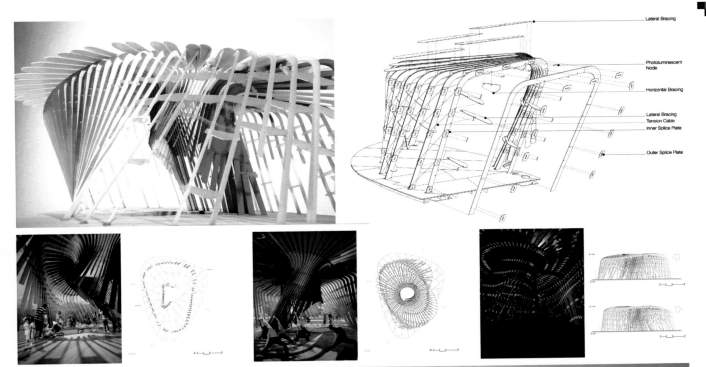

Lateral Bracing

Photoluminescent
Node

Horizontal Bracing

Lateral Bracing
Tension Cable
Inner Splice Plate

Outer Splice Plate

Club de Fútbol Monterrey

Michael Westlake, Alan Tansey - *Populous, United States*
Ian Keough, Joe White - *Buro happold, United States*

The project is for a 50,000 seat soccer stadium in Monterrey, Mexico. The design of the roof geometry involved close coordination with the Architect (Populous), Structural Engineer (Buro Happold), and cladding manufacturer; in order to do this a variety of software platforms were used involving Rhino, Grasshopper, Revit, and Robot. Parametric models and scripting techniques were utilized in order to share information and develop an iterative design approach.

The roof geometry had three objectives: first, to shelter the spectators and enhance the crowd atmosphere; second, to allow vistas to nearby topography (the Cerro de la Silla mountain range) to create a local awareness whilst still in the stadium; last, to allow sufficient natural ventilation within the concourse area through the use of openings, 'gills' along the upper edge of the roof. The gills encourage airflow within the upper concourse area of the stadium.

CFD analysis was performed in order to check that the design allowed sufficient airflow in this area to prevent heat build up and keep thermal comfort within an acceptable range.

Once the initial concept was finalized and the principles of the geometry understood, a parametric model was built in grasshopper to aid form finding and refinement of the roof design. During this process, the Rhino surface was shared between the architect and the structural engineer where structural feedback could be given. The overall form of the building could be adjusted using law curves that represented key points of the roof geometry. Using these law curves the form could be broadly sculpted and then checked against site constraints, structure and ultimately aesthetics. The gill opening and length could be controlled by adjusting the perpendicular dimension between the upper and lower curve of the opening.

In order to support an iterative design workflow, it was necessary for the structural engineer to create software which would convert the Rhino surface geometry provided by the architect into a structural center line model. The software is a stand-alone executable using the Rhino API to interface with Populous' geometry. Using Populous' Rhino model of the facade of the stadium, Buro Happold were able to generate full three dimensional trusses of the roof.

The software then laid out the trusses in a 2D array for checking by the engineer. This visual inspection acted as a first check of the inputs of the tool. The structural centerlines were then imported directly into Revit as solid elements for documentation and into Robot for structural analysis. Automating the creation of the structural geometry allowed Buro Happold to respond quickly to changes in the architectural form.

The cladding for the roof is a standing seam aluminum system that is able to follow the double curvature of the roof design. This was achieved by utilizing three different types of sheeting, straight, tapered, and specially formed sheets. Areas in the roof where the curvature was too high had to be claded with the specially formed sheets that were designed for specific positions on the roof. In order to make the design economically viable, the design team worked with the cladding manufacturer to reduce the amount of specialized sheeting required by adapting the form to the characteristics of the product. The cladding manufacturer analyzed the rhino surface to calculate the type of cladding required; this analysis was then used to adapt the parametric model to optimize the scheme. Several iterations of the process resulted in a reduction in cost of over 50% from the initial form.

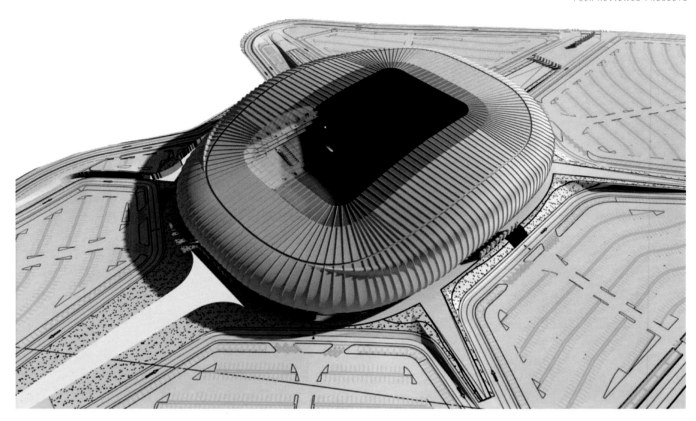

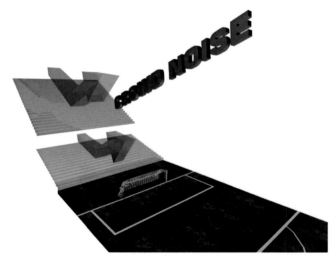

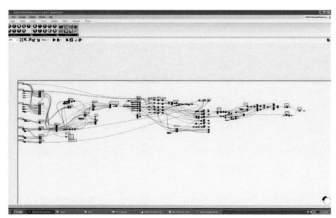

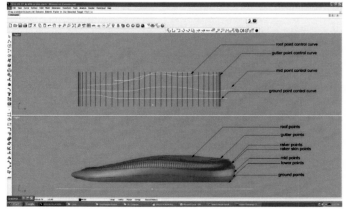

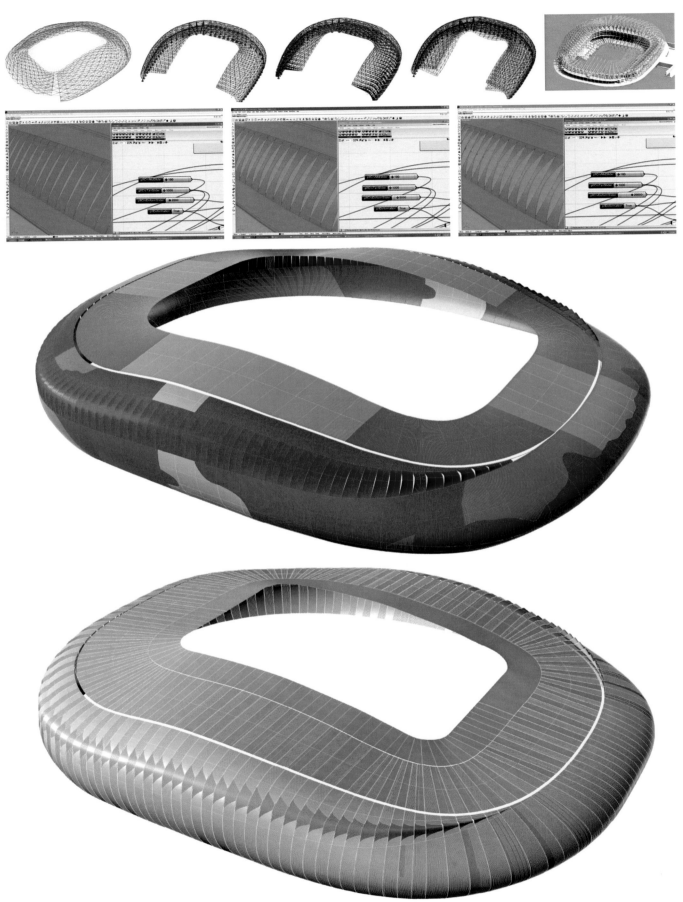

Contested Boundaries

Joseph Choma - *architectuREdefined / Massachusetts Institute of Technology, United States*

In order for one to design, one must have constraints. These constraints give designers a new born freedom to design within. Instrumentality is when the designer embodies the tool as a mechanism to generate unpredictable new ideas. Often times, designers begin to work within a given medium without explicitly acknowledging how such embedded constraints will influence their design process. The experience and consequences associated with digital instrumentation will yield different results than those emerging out of physical material manipulations. A digitally driven design may be seamlessly precise and consistent but may also feel sterile and distant from the human body. A materially driven design may be intimate and tactile but may lack the accuracy needed to connect elements. This research investigates the relationship between efficiency, precision and tactile variation within architectural design and fabrication. Digital fabrication techniques are combined with hand craft material manipulations in search of a unique hybrid tectonic that merges connection accuracies with subtle but sensual divergences between repeating modules. Prototypes are being constructed at the object, installation, and architectural scale. Our project documents the challenges associated with translating a consistent material process in each stage of this research.

A current alternative fabrication process is in progress. The challenges associated with translating a digital model into a physical manifestation is being documented within this research. The next prototype will match a significantly closer resemblance to the digital models of instability.

This research does not claim to have developed a "better" fabrication process, but rather asks the question, how do we qualify fabrication processes in our current discourse? A hybrid fabrication process which combines digital fabrication with hand craft techniques suggests an alternative approach to current fabrication trends— automation and optimization. Perhaps, a slightly slower process which yields a sensibility to intimacy is something to be considered.

fig 1: The boundary of a cube is redefined with a volume packed geodesic order, which is embedded with fan vault modules. Alternative parameters of instability are portrayed.

fig 2: The overlapping layers of the three dimensional embedding process.

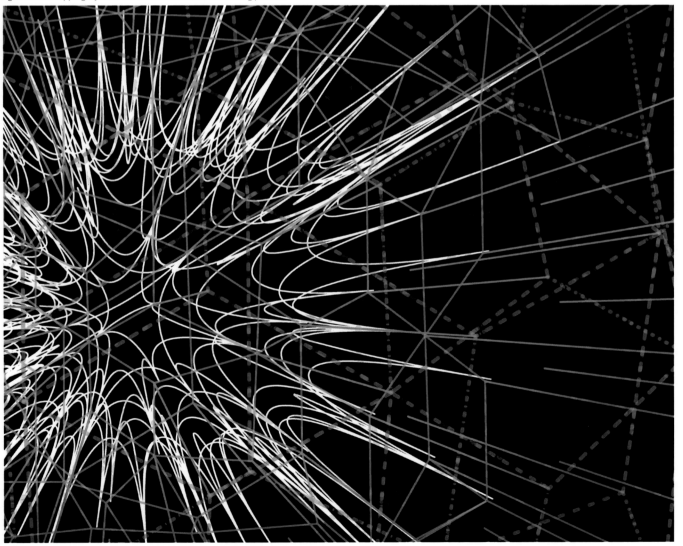

fig 3: The order in which cells are transformed into surfaces is important for complex patterns, especially when each surface logic has an inherent algorithmic grain and needs to maintain matching edge conditions with its neighbors.

fig 4: Volume packing structure where vaults radiate around a common center point.

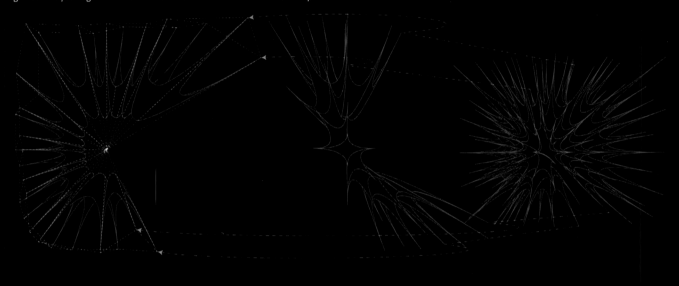

fig 5: Exploding a strip of volume packing vaults to examine the spatial boundaries defined by the outer quill-like edges compared to the synclastic inner curvatures.

Fig 6: Conceptualizing how the inner and outer boundaries defined by the vaults and spikes could extend to frame more than one global geometry. The outer boundary no longer has to be an offset of the inner.

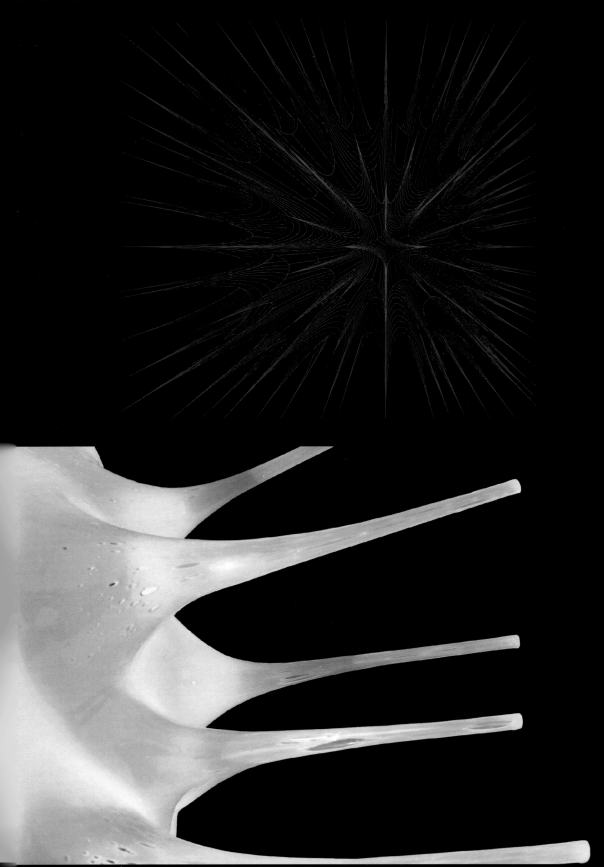

Detroit SuperDivision

David Freeland, Brennan Buck - *Freeland Buck, United States*
David Fletcher - *David Fletcher Studio, United States*

In order for one to design, one must have constraints. These constraints give designers a new born freedom to design within. Instrumentality is when the designer embodies the tool as a mechanism to generate unpredictable new ideas. Often times, designers begin to work within a given medium without explicitly acknowledging how such embedded constraints will influence their design process. The experience and consequences associated with digital instrumentation will yield different results than those emerging out of physical material manipulations. A digitally driven design may be seamlessly precise and consistent but may also feel sterile and distant from the human body. A materially driven design may be intimate and tactile but may lack the accuracy needed to connect elements. This research investigates the relationship between efficiency, precision and tactile variation within architectural design and fabrication. Digital fabrication techniques are combined with hand craft material manipulations in search of a unique hybrid tectonic that merges connection accuracies with subtle but sensual divergences between repeating modules. Prototypes are being constructed at the object, installation, and architectural scale. Our project documents the challenges associated with translating a consistent material process in each stage of this research.

A current alternative fabrication process is in progress. The challenges associated with translating a digital model into a physical manifestation is being documented within this research. The next prototype will match a significantly closer resemblance to the digital models of instability.

This research does not claim to have developed a "better" fabrication process, but rather asks the question, how do we qualify fabrication processes in our current discourse? A hybrid fabrication process which combines digital fabrication with hand craft techniques suggests an alternative approach to current fabrication trends— automation and optimization. Perhaps, a slightly slower process which yields a sensibility to intimacy is something to be considered.

Hedgerow Sections

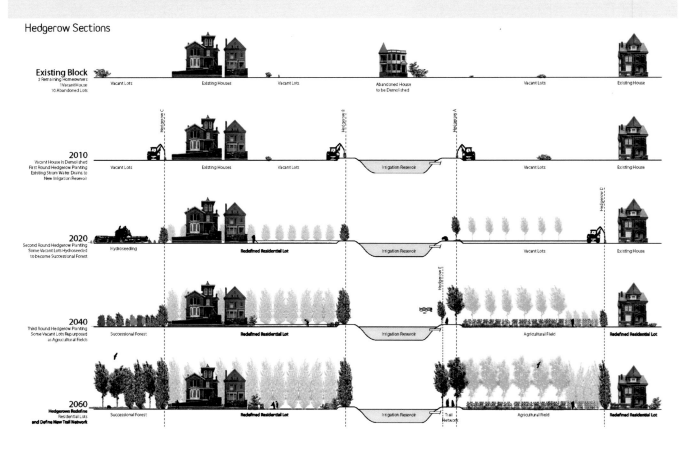

Superdivision Algorithm

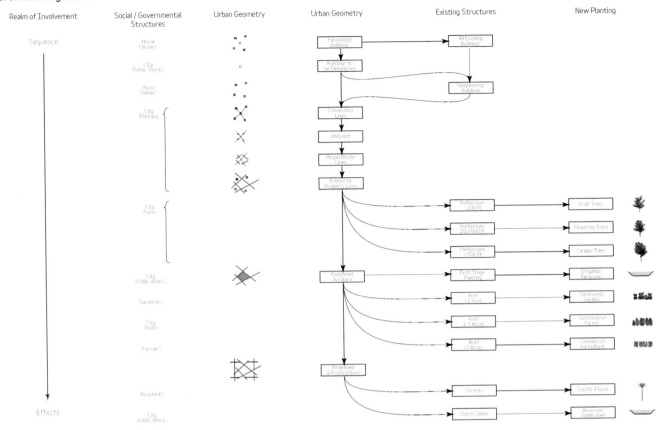

Realm of Involvement	Social / Governmental Structures	Urban Geometry	Urban Geometry	Existing Structures	New Planting

Sequence

Effects

Property Ownership

Detroit: Dense Vacancy

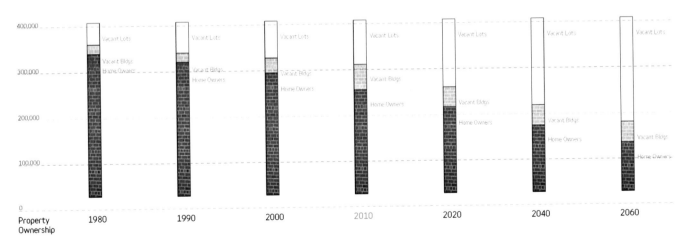

1980 1990 2000 2010 2020 2040 2060

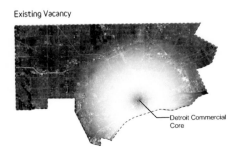

Existing Vacancy

Detroit Commercial Core

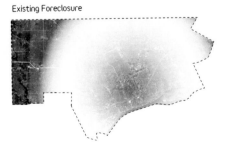

Existing Foreclosure

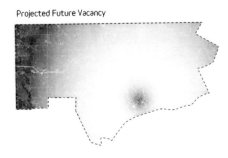

Projected Future Vacancy

Hedgerow Geometry

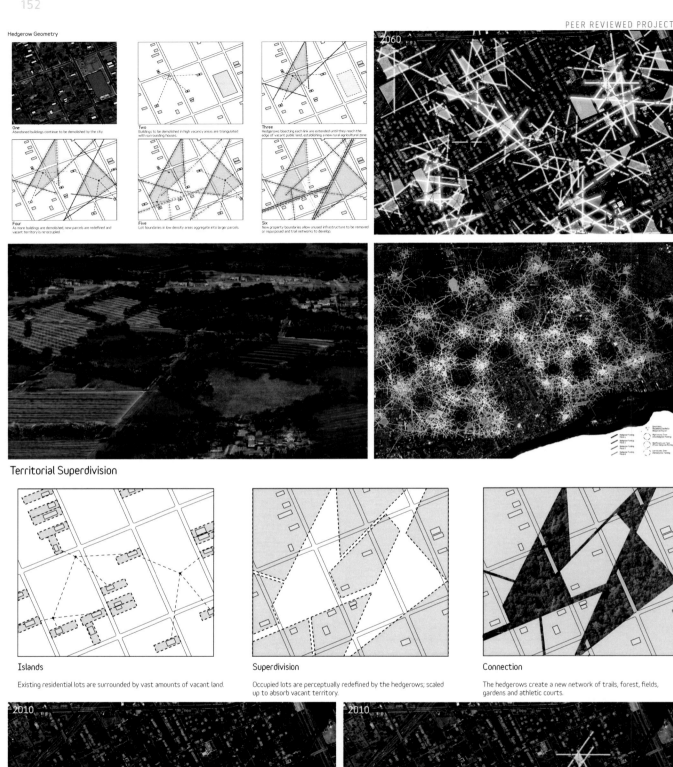

One
Abandoned buildings continue to be demolished by the city.

Two
Buildings to be demolished in high vacancy areas are triangulated with surrounding houses.

Three
Hedgerows bisecting each link are extended until they reach the edge of vacant public land, establishing a new rural agricultural zone

Four
As more buildings are demolished, new parcels are redefined and vacant territory is re-occupied.

Five
Lot boundaries in low density areas aggregate into larger parcels.

Six
New property boundaries allow unused infrastructure to be removed or repurposed and trail networks to develop.

2060

Territorial Superdivision

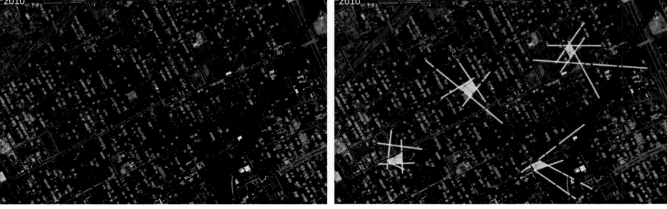

Islands

Existing residential lots are surrounded by vast amounts of vacant land.

Superdivision

Occupied lots are perceptually redefined by the hedgerows; scaled up to absorb vacant territory.

Connection

The hedgerows create a new network of trails, forest, fields, gardens and athletic courts.

2010

2010

2020

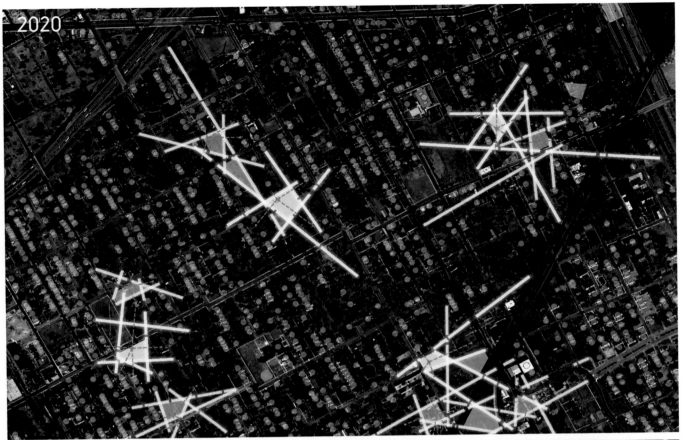

2040

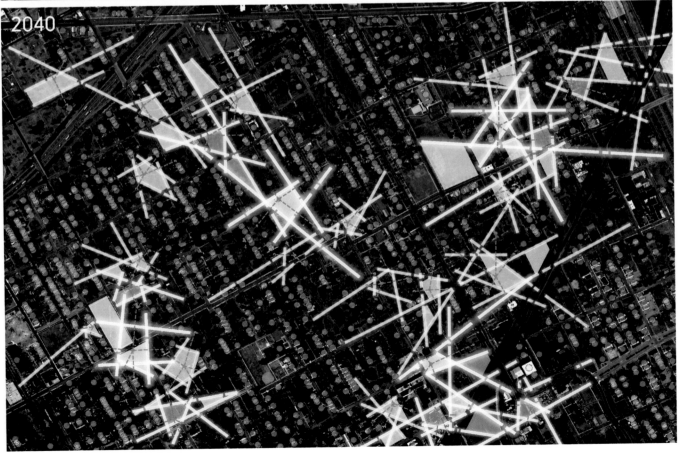

Rhythm and Resolution

Matias del Campo, Sandra Manninger - *SPAN, Austria*

Beauty of style and harmony and grace and good rhythm depend on simplicity
- Plato

Modes of Material Aggregation

Within the discipline of architectural production, the matter of rhythm can be considered an inherent condition dealing with modes of material aggregation. In any extent, architecture can be considered a form of art that deals with the aggregation and organization of matter in order to create spatial differentiation between interior and exterior as well as dealing with concepts of compartmentalization. These methods, of accumulating matter in architecture, have been discussed extensively within the discourse, following schemes to create integrated bodies. Bodies that follow specific regulations of proportion, scale and symmetry, have been the main focus of discussion; following specific techniques of order, they present an idea of thinking in complete and whole bodies, with defined boundary conditions of stabile nature. This essay however tries to include a novel perspective to the part to whole relationship idea by including the topics of rhythm & resolution.

Resolution

Resolution in this debate is defined as the process of making individual components of an object distinguishable. This differentiation is dependent of the scale and observation distance, rendering a body comprised of components into a surface, in accordance to the relation of the size of its parts to the entire figuration. In this plane of thinking resolution is considered to be an inherent quality in the packing or tiling of articulated formations into stable lattices, resulting in unstable and opulent spatial conditions widely present in the work of contemporary, computational design orientated practices.

In 1993, Moby released a record entitled Thousand. The track starts with a beat of around 120BPM (Beats Per Minute) and rises to the 1000BPM mentioned in the title. What happens in the process is that the beat of the track transforms from a strictly defined stable and discrete condition to a continuous, seamless sound texture. In this case rhythm and resolution form an intricate bonding condition, which can be described as a parametric state, as the individual elements of the array form an interconnected and interdependent lattice of relationships, resulting in funky spatial conditions. Components, rhythms, intervals, and resolution include an inherent set of orders that can be combined with each other, resulting in surprising affects generated by gradient transitions between the described conditions. This could reach from seamless changes in the scale of components, to continuous material transformation to the application of gradient chromatic effects on surfaces. One example,that deals with the idea of small-scale components as a constituting element of a surface condition, is the Austrian Pavilion for the Expo in Shanghai in 2010 that bears a micro-tiling façade built up of hexagonal components.

The small scale off the components result in a smooth and even surface, bearing the already discussed possibilities in creating gradient colorations. However, if we observe the described effect in the track Thousand and speculate upon its inherent opportunities in the discipline of architecture, it would describe a possible shift in the notion of using components as a single constituting element of a surface and embrace an opportunity where components oscillate between coarse surface population and finely meshed material behavior. This constitutes a gradient transition between structure and material, thus becoming a continuous seamless moment of transition between basic architectural facets. The opportunities inherent in contemporary software packages to create flows of interaction between nodes, in order to create highly intricate relationships between components, have produced specific plateaus of thinking within the speculations on rhythm and resolution.

(fig. 3) Austrian Pavilion Shanghai Expo 2010 (Photo© Maria Ziegelböck 2010)

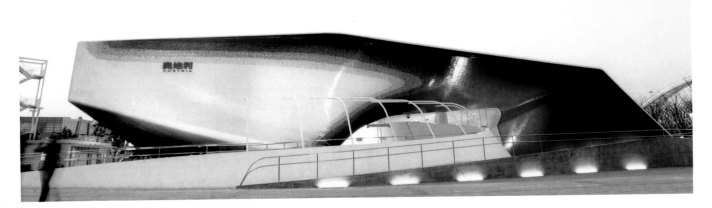

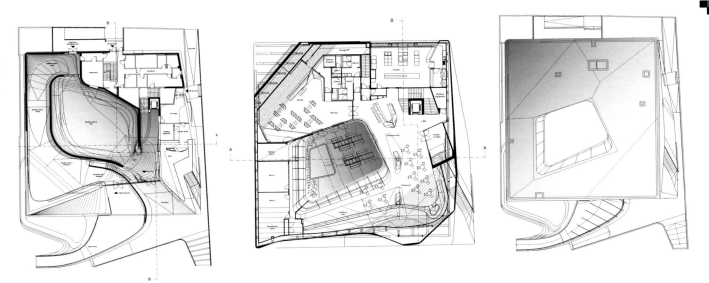

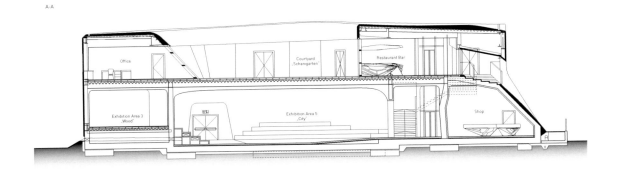

A-A

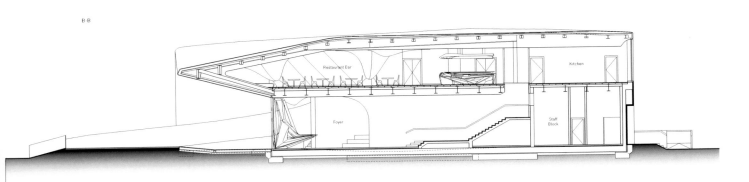

B-B

Nanotectonica

Jonas Coersmeier - *Pratt Institute, United States*

Keywords: Nanotectonica super-human senses algorithmic deeper natural systems electron microscopy parametric modelling digital fabrication architectural design nanotechnology biological living material properties gravity generative drawing SEM species prototyping digital installation.

Nanotectonica is an ongoing research project that pairs super-human senses with algorithmic tools for a deeper understanding of natural systems. Electron microscopy, parametric modeling, and digital fabrication are integrated into an experimental, architectural design process.

The research is conducted in the context of design studios and production seminars, and it is supported by industry partners, who provide essential expertise, access, and equipment in the field of nanotechnology.

Nanotechnology and algorithmic tools enable expanded and deeper investigations into natural structures. At the same time, a new understanding of living systems emerges. The search is not limited to the phenotypical expressions of nature, but seeks to decipher its organizing principles. The analytical routines of an evolved scientific method allow us to speculate on the underlying systems of biological processes. Beyond the bionic, which idealizes living structures as resolved and completed systems, and beyond biomimicry, which strives to copy those systems in their full complexity, we are in search of procedurally optimized building methods and structural concepts employed in living systems.

At nanoscale, the material properties of organizations change. Gravity is no longer the dominant force when the size of the system radically decreases. The Scanning Electron Microscope (SEM) allows glimpses into organizational systems that work beyond the logic of primary gravitational considerations.

While focusing on analysis and design production, the research bases its exploration in the context of recent architectural history. The search for structural precedents in nature is as old as the history of architecture itself, with Functionalism, Constructivism, and Natural Symbolism as clear expressions of that search. In its quest for natural prototypes, early Modernism found its inspiration in the work of Raoul H. Francé, among others. In the later twentieth century Fuller, Ricolait, and Frei Otto were interested in the processural in nature. In the age of advanced computation and nano technology, their methods of optimization invite re-examination and further development.

The procedural operations of the scanning electron microscope are followed by generative drawing and fabrication techniques that analyze, process, and enhance the source material. Digital output models inform structural and tectonic propositions that are tested in the context of full scale installations. The process chain includes the following phases: SEM imaging > species taxonomy > analytical drawing > generative drawing > parametric modeling > prototyping > digital fabrication > installation.

The installation was developed at the Digital Design Department, G. Professor Jonas Coersmeier, University Kassel, during the summer of 2009. Participating students: Giampiero Riggio, Roberta Ragonese, Ljuba Tascheva, Jan Weissenfeldt, Pat Taylor, Katja Pape, Rania Abdurahman, Christina Finke, Shahram Abbasian, Michael Quickert.

10kV, 900x,

⊢ 20 µm ⊣

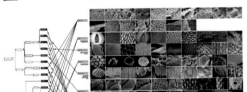

NANOPOOL nanotectonica ws 2008/09

Natural probe drawings

Analysis of the pseudotrachaeas system

Sem labellum_natural system

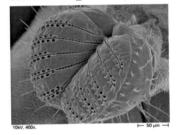

10kV, 400x,   ⊢ 50 µm ⊣

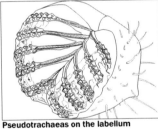

10kV, 700x,   ⊢ 30 µm ⊣

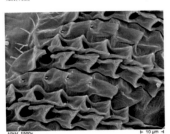

10kV, 1500x,   ⊢ 10 µm ⊣

Natural drawings

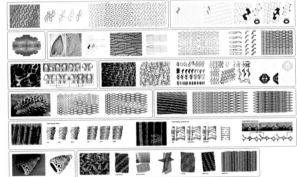

Pseudotrachaeas on the labellum

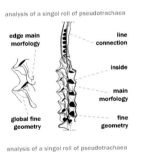

Detail (front view)

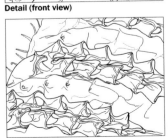

Detail (side view)

three pseudotrachaeas lines

- three connection lines
- natural curvature
- line system

analysis of a singol roll of pseudotrachaea

- edge main morfology
- line connection
- inside
- main morfology
- global fine geometry
- fine geometry

analysis of a singol roll of pseudotrachaea

- global fine geometry
- edge fine geometry
- connection points

semplification

pseudotrachaes distribution on teh labellum surface

geometrical main axes

semplification

- alternating openings and exterior surfaces

simplification of form

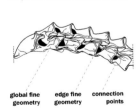

semplification and schematization

- main morfology
- geometrical main axes

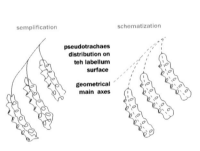

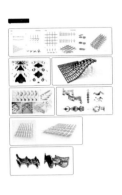

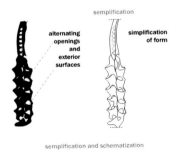

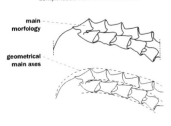

schematization

Natural probe drawings
Analysis of the natural detail of the pseudotrachaeas

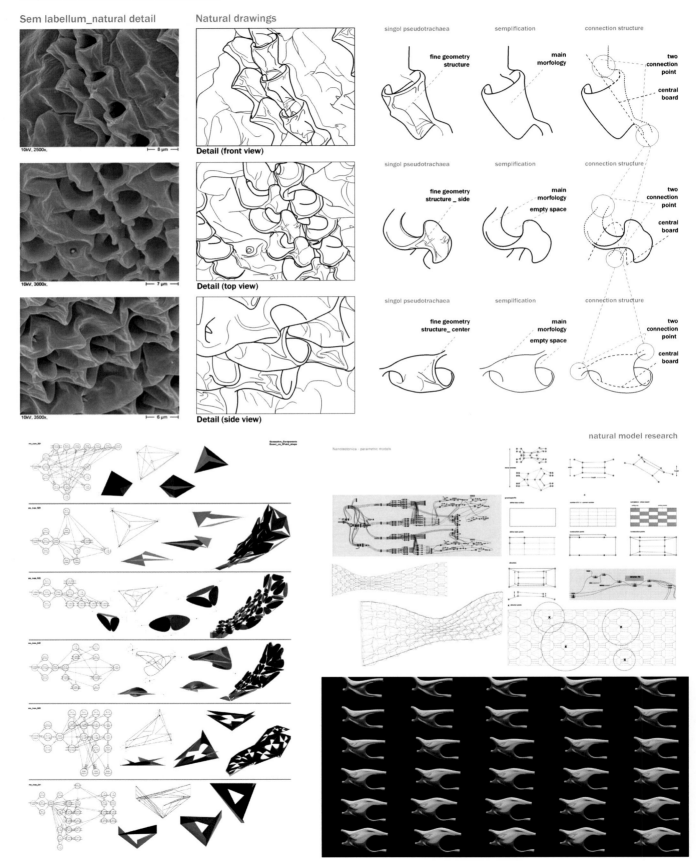

Sem labellum_natural detail

Natural drawings

Detail (front view)

Detail (top view)

Detail (side view)

singol pseudotrachaea — semplification — connection structure

natural model research

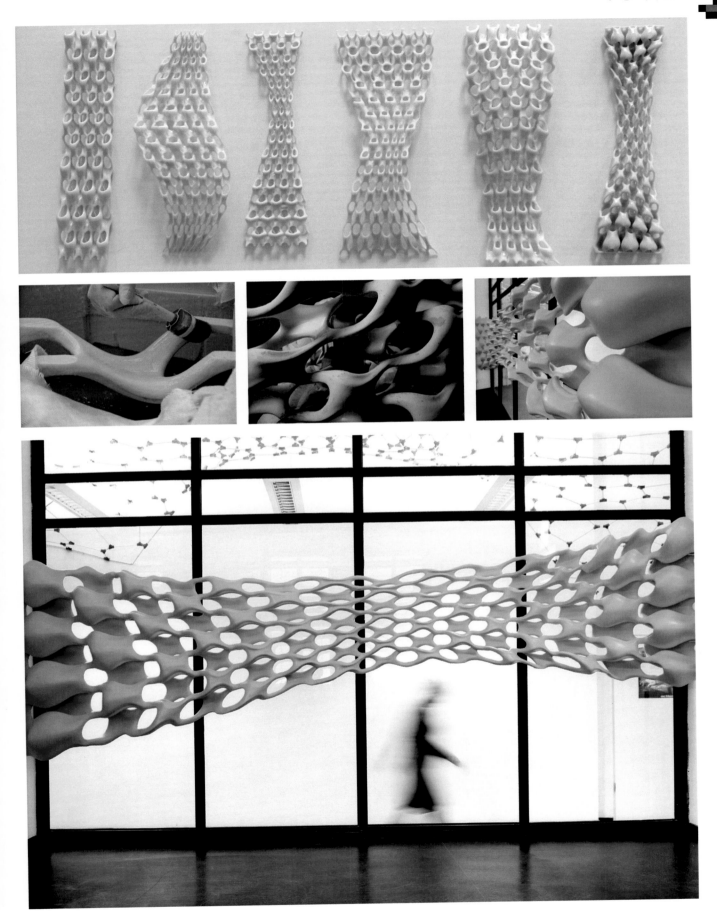

Biographies

Biographies

Conference Chairs

Aaron Sprecher

Aaron Sprecher is co-founder and partner of Open Source Architecture (*www.o-s-a.com*). He completed his graduate studies at the University of California at Los Angeles. His research and design work focuses on the synergy between information technologies, computational languages, and automated digital systems, examining the way in which technology informs and generates innovative approaches to design processes. Beside numerous publications and exhibitions, he has lectured in many institutions including MIT (In-fluence Af-fluence Con-fluence | Notes on N-dimensional Architecture), RISD (n-Natures | Fibrous Morphologies), and Harvard University GSD (Intensity, Extensity and Potentiality | A few Notes on Information and the Architectural Organism). Aaron Sprecher is co-curator and co-editor of the groundbreaking exhibition and publication The Gen(H)ome Project (MAK Center, Los Angeles, 2006) and design curator of Performalism (Tel Aviv Museum of Art, 2008). He is a recipient of numerous research grants, most recently, awarded with a Canada Foundation for Innovation award. Aaron Sprecher is currently Assistant Professor at McGill University School of Architecture and a visiting Tutor at the Architectural Association.

Shai Yeshayahu

Shai Yeshayahu is an Associate Professor, at Southern Illinois University of Carbondale in Architecture, Digital design, Fabrication and Design foundation. He received his MArch from Ohio State University, Knowlton School of Architecture; BSAT from New York Institute of Technology; and has studied linguistics and art history at the Fundación Ortega y Gasset. In 2006, he founded the Digital Fabrication Lab, df_Lab@ SIUC as part of an initiative to implement a digital culture across the curriculum. In 2007 he co-chaired and curated '[A]esthesia,' a symposium and exhibit about the relation of the senses to digital practices. He is the co-founder of VerS, a research and design practice responsive to how ancient, emerging, and local data informs making. The office has built, exhibited, and published in Latin America, Canada, Israel, and the UK. The scope of his professional activities ranges from academic research, international competitions, installations, exhibits, and private commissions.

Pablo Lorenzo-Eiroa

Pablo Lorenzo-Eiroa has been integrating theory and profession with work ranging from academic research through scholarships and publications, to professional architecture design in private and state commissions through EIROA ARCHITECTS. His projects develop analog and digital strategies, as continuous and discontinuous signs of information, through different media-based interfaces that recognize but critique the most stable canonical structures through topological transformations to overcome the predetermination of types and departing organizational structures. He has introduced these concepts at The Cooper Union to integrate the legacy of hand craft and a deep understanding of innovative architecture representation within contemporary digital strategies and toward the autonomy of digital space. His recently published *Instalaciones: Sobre el trabajo de Peter Eisenman* includes theoretical discussions on Eisenman's installations after his collaboration on more than ten projects. Mr. Lorenzo-Eiroa is a Fulbright and National Endowment for the Arts scholar, alumni from Princeton University and the University of Buenos Aires. He is currently Associate Professor Adjunct of architecture, head professor of design II and advanced digital studies at The Cooper Union both at the graduate and undergraduate levels. He has lectured in many institutions worldwide, is the recipient of many scholarships and design awards, and has published in different media. *www.eiroaarchitects.com*

Exhibition Chairs

Chandler Ahrens

Chandler Ahrens completed his studies with an M. Arch. from the University of California Los Angeles in 2002 and received a B. Arch. from Savannah College of Art and Design in 1995. He co-founded Open Source Architecture in 2004 and remains a director of the Los Angeles office. He has worked for several international firms, including 8 years at Morphosis Architects. He was responsible for content and installation of an exhibition on the New Academic Building for Cooper Union in New York, 2005. In 2006, he was a co-curator of the Gen(h)ome Project at the MAK Center for Art and Architecture. In 2008, he coordinated content and supervised installation of the Performalism exhibition in Tel Aviv. In addition, he has lectured at various academic institutions and is frequently a guest critic at universities around Los Angeles.

Axel Schmitzberger

Axel Schmitzberger is currently teaching as Associate Professor at California State Polytechnic University. Prior to this engagement, he has taught at various academic institutions both in Los Angeles in the areas of Architecture, Multimedia, and Graphic Design. He received his architectural master degree from the Vienna University of Technology, Austria, and practiced in various architectural design offices on internationally recognized projects. In 1999, he founded hostcell to pursue interdisciplinary projects with wide recognition, such as the interior design for the Austrian national broadcast agency ORF, and has been recognized for his contribution and to +rosebud magazine.

After his reallocation to the United States and a three year engagement with Morphosis Architects, he founded and currently manages the practice 11.1 design | research along with partner Arshia Mahmoodi, exploring contemporary built architecture at all scales; the firms most recent project is the construction of a high-end in residence in Hollywood Hills. In 2009, his firm hostcell transformed into the graphic design enterprise starfish-prime as a collaboration in contemporary graphic design with partner Ice Lee. He is currently featured in the forthcoming book Material Matter, by editors Michael Meredith and Gail borden.

Michael Wen-Sen Su

Visiting Assistant Professor, Pratt Institute
Michael Su holds a B.S. from Caltech, M.S. from Columbia University, B.Arch. from The Cooper Union School of Architecture, and M.A. from Princeton University. At Princeton University, he is currently completing a dissertation on the interchange between science and architecture in the early works of R. Buckminster Fuller. He is also a Visiting Adjunct Professor at the Pratt Institute School of Architecture, where he is Coordinator and Instructor of the Undergraduate Degree Project. His particular research and design interest is on the notion of "Sensory Architecture", i.e. – architectural practices and theories which explicitly incorporate and process the informational content of the senses.

Nancy Yen-wen Cheng
Acadia President

Associate Professor Nancy Yen-wen Cheng, RA, LEED AP, is Director of University of Oregon's Portland Architecture Program where she teaches architectural design and computer methods. She researches how digital tools shape design thinking. She is interested in maximizing creative engagement through sketching, handcraft, and material properties combined with sophisticated modeling and machine processes. Since teaching at the University of Hong Kong in 1993-96, Nancy has studied how the Internet can foster learning communities. She is working with the Inter/National Coalition for Electronic Portfolio Research to explore how Web 2.0 tools can support development of communication and collaboration skills. Her students have worked with Oregon intentional communities to envision sustainable housing.

Professor Cheng is President of the Association of Computer Aided Design in Architecture (ACADIA) in 2010-2011. She chaired the national American Institute of Architects' Technology in Architectural Practice group in 2004, co-chaired a Fabrication conference in Toronto, and has edited issues of the International Journal of Architectural Computing.

Prior to teaching in Hong Kong, she worked for Boston architectural firms such as Kallmann, McKinnell and Wood and Raphael Moneo. She holds a bachelor's degree from Yale University and a master's degree from Harvard Graduate School of Design.
http://eportfolio.uoregon.edu/Members/nyc

SPECIALTIES:
media and design process, internet collaborations, digital design teaching

Exhibition Datamining, Co-Design
John Carpenter is an artist and designer who uses immersive, interactive installations to explore how people interact with complex spaces. Based in Santa Monica, he works for Morphosis Architects (2005-present) as the Visual and Interactive Designer, and teaches at Loyola Marymount University. John earned his MFA from the Department of Design | Media Arts at UCLA (2009) where his thesis work, Shoreline Equivalent: Qualitative Spaces in Interactive Art, uses qualitative observations of sand patterns at the beach to convey the fluid, dynamic, and emergent nature of the shoreline.

Curated Projects (in order of Appearance)

Ruy Klein

Ruy Klein examines contemporary design problems at the intersection of architecture, nature, and technology. The devastating technological changes of the last century have opened up new territories where artificial and natural systems share vague boundaries. As architecture grapples with new synthetic domains, Ruy Klein pursues new possibilities for design by negotiating the uncertainties of a contemporary material practice radically altered by technology. Over the past decade, Ruy Klein has conducted a sequence of projects focused on the advancement of new design technologies in conjunction with the cultivation of new aesthetic experiences and a renegotiation of architecture's meaning structures. The mutual imbrications of historically incompatible material regimes govern the sensibility of the work where attention is fixed on the sublime horizon that is now interlaced with feral technologies.

Ruy Klein is widely published and exhibited. Winner of multiple design awards and recognized internationally as one the foremost speculative practices in architecture today, the practice is currently pursuing completion of its first building commissions while continuing its extended research into digital fabrication. The directors, David Ruy and Karel Klein are both currently teaching at the Pratt Institute GAUD.

www.ruyklein.com

Directors:
David Ruy , *david@ruyklein.com*
Karel Klein, *karel@ruyklein.com*

Andrew Saunders

Andrew Saunders is an Assistant Professor of Architecture at Rensselaer Polytechnic Institute in New York. He received his Masters in Architecture from the Harvard Graduate School of Design. He has significant professional experience as project designer for Eisenman Architects, Leeser Architecture, and Preston Scott Cohen, Inc. He has taught and guest lectured at a variety of institutions, including Cooper Union and the Cranbrook Academy of Art. In 2004, he was awarded the SOM Research and Traveling Fellowship for Masters of Architecture to pursue his research on the relationship of equation based geometries to early 20th century pioneers in reinforced concrete. His current practice and research interests lie in computational geometry as it relates to emerging technology, fabrication, and performance. He is currently working on a book using parametric modeling as an analysis tool of 17th century Italian Baroque architecture.

Ferda Kolatan & Erich Schoenenberger
su11 architecture+design

Ferda Kolatan and Erich Schoenenberger co-founded su11 architecture+design in New York City in 1999. Since then, they have received the Swiss National Culture Award for Art and Design and the ICFF Editors Award for 'Best New Designer' in 2001. In 2006,they were selected finalists for the prestigious Chernikhov Price and in 2008 they were chosen as finalists for the MoMA/PS1 YAP competition. In 2010, su11 was invited to collaborate in a "Journey to Zero", an initiative to envision a future Zero Emission world sponsored by Nissan and guided by TED founder Richard Saul Wurman.

Their work has been published nationally and internationally including the NY Times, LA Times, Washington Post, Le Monde, AD, Archilab's Futurehouse, Space, Monitor, L'Arca, Arch+, New New York, PreFAb Modern, Digital Real, The Metapolis Dictionary of Advanced Architecture, and Dwell. They have also been exhibited at venues such as the Museum of Modern Art, Walker Art Center, Art Center College of Design, Vitra Design Museum, PS1, Artists Space NY, Archilab Orleans, Documenta X, Art Basel, Siggraph 2009 and the Carnegie Museum of Art.

Ferda Kolatan was born in Cologne, Germany. He received his Architectural Diploma with distinction from the RWTH Aachen in 1993 and his Masters in Architecture from Columbia University in 1995, where he received the Lucille Smyser Lowenfish Memorial Price and the Honor Award for Excellence in Design. Ferda Kolatan has taught at Columbia University, RPI, UBC, and the RWTH Aachen. He is currently a Senior Lecturer at the University of Pennsylvania and a Visiting Adjunct Professor at Pratt Institute in New York. He is also Senior Researcher for the NSO headed by Cecil Balmond at Penn Design.

Erich Schoenenberger, R.A. AIA was born in St. Gallen, Switzerland. He received his Bachelor of Environmental Design at Tech.School of Nova Scotia in 1993 in Halifax, Canada and his Masters in Architecture from Columbia University in 1995. He worked for Kol/Mac Studio in New York, as a Senior Designer from 1995 to 1997. In this period,he was the Project Architect for the O/K Apartment, which has been published widely, receiving awards, and being exhibited, among other places, at MoMA as part of the Un-Private House Show. Currently he is also a Visiting Instructor at Pratt Institute.
www.su11.com

Omar Khan

Omar Khan completed his post-professional studies at the Massachusetts Institute of Technology and his professional studies at Cornell University. He is an associate professor in the Department of Architecture at the University at Buffalo. His research and practice address responsiveness and performativity in architecture. In 1995, in collaboration with Laura Garofalo, he established Liminal Projects, a practice that has developed performance spaces for artists, interactive and responsive installations, domestic interiors, and award winning competitions. Their work has been exhibited at The Kitchen, NYC; The Whitney Annex, NYC; The Urban Center, NYC; The Storefront for Art and Architecture, NYC and The National Building Museum, Washington DC among others. They were winners in the Architectural League of New York's Young Architects Forum 1999. Prof. Khan has received grants from the Rockefeller Foundation, New York State Council for the Arts, and the Department of Education and is a 2008 fellow of the New York Foundation for the Arts. Prof. Khan is a past editor for the Journal of Architectural Education (JAE) and currently a co-editor of the *www.situatedtechnologies.net/?q=node/75* Situated Technologies Pamphlet Series, published by the Architectural League of New York. At the University at Buffalo, he co-directs the cast.ap.buffalo.edu/ Center for Architecture and Situated Technologies where his research includes transitive materials, responsive architecture and situated technologies.

Mark Shepard

Mark Shepard is an artist, architect, and researcher whose work addresses new social spaces and signifying structures of contemporary network cultures. His current research investigates the implications of mobile and pervasive computing for architecture and urbanism. Recent works include Hertzian Rain, a variable event structure designed to raise awareness of issues surrounding the wireless topography of urban environments through telematic conversations based on sound and bodily movement, and the Tactical Sound Garden [TSG], an open source software platform for cultivating virtual sound gardens in urban public space, which has been presented at museums, festivals, and arts events internationally. He recently curated the "Toward the Sentient City," an exhibition organized by the Architectural League of New York that critically explored the evolving relationship between ubiquitous computing, architecture, and the future of urban space, and is one of the editors of the Situated Technologies Pamphlets Series. Mark is an Assistant Professor of Architecture and Media Study at the University at Buffalo, State University of New York, where he co-directs the Center for Architecture and Situated Technologies and coordinates the media | architecture | computing program.

Paul Vanouse

Paul Vanouse has been working in emerging media forms since 1990. Interdisciplinarity and impassioned amateurism guide his art practice. His electronic cinema, biological experiments, and interactive installations have been exhibited in over 20 countries and widely across the US.

Venues have included: Walker Art Center in Minneapolis, New Museum in New York, Museo Nacional de Bellas Artes in Buenos Aires, Louvre in Paris, NGBK in Berlin, Zentrum fur Kunst und Medientechnologie in Karlsruhe, Centre de Cultura Contemporania in Barcelona, and TePapa Museum in Wellington, New Zealand. Vanouse's work has been supported by Creative Capital Foundation, Renew Media (Rockefeller) Foundation, New York State Council on the Arts, New York Foundation for the Arts, Sun Microsystems, Pennsylvania Council on the Arts, Heinz Foundation, Mellon Charitable Trust, and National Science Foundation. His work has garnered prizes at international competitions including ARS Electronica in Austria and VIDA in Spain.

Paul Vanouse is an Associate Professor of Visual Studies at the University at Buffalo, where he co-Directs the Emerging Practices MFA concentration. His current project, "Latent Figure Protocol," uses molecular biology techniques to challenge "genome-hype" and to confront issues surrounding DNA fingerprinting.

Michael Meredith, Hillary Sample - MOS

Michael Meredith is an Associate Professor at Harvard University, Graduate School of Design. Hilary Sample is an Associate Professor at Yale University School of Architecture. They are the principals of MOS. MOS's built projects include PS1/MoMA Afterparty, an artist studio for Terry Winters, and a series of installations and collaborations with artists. Since they began their office, they have been developing real-time physics software that utilizes video game engines to produce form-finding. This software produces a design environment that exists between the "digital" and the "real," in which they can experiment with architectural form. In 2010, they received an Academy Award from the American Academy of Arts and Letters.
www.mos-office.net

Mark Linder, Julia Czerniak - Clear, McLain Clutter

McLain Clutter is an architect, writer and Assistant Professor at University of Michigan Taubman College of Architecture and Urban Planning. His design work has been exhibited internationally and his recent essays have appeared in Grey Room and MONU. Clutter's current work explores how media and technological methods of imaging urbanism working epistemologically to prohibit or promote design strategies and construct urban publics and subjectivities.

Mark Linder is an Associate Professor at Syracuse University. His research explores issues of transdisciplinarity: approaches that simultaneously affirm disciplinary knowledge and attenuate disciplinary limits, and that enable architects to engage constituencies, operate in contexts, and address problems that are traditionally understood as only marginal to architecture. He is the author of Nothing Less than Literal: Architecture after Minimalism, and his writings have appeared in Assemblage, AA Files, ANY, Architecture + Urbanism, Design Book Review, Documents, Harvard Design Review, Hunch, Journal of Architectural Education, and Log. He has lectured throughout the United States and Europe, and with Julia Czerniak, is a principal of CLEAR, a collaborative practice conceived as an framework to encompass scholarship and design work.

Buro Happold

David is a Principal of Buro Happold with the specific responsibility of leading the environmental, sustainability, and MEP design group in Los Angeles. His design philosophy is that successful environmental design is achieved through influencing the architectural language, form, function, and fabric of a building, masterplan, or landscape to minimize the environmental impact of energy, water, material, and waste. Always challenging – never accepting convention. With a career spanning over 20 years, he has been involved in many urban planning, cultural / civic, transportation, commercial, hotel and residential projects, both in the U.S, UK, and globally. He is a guest lecturer on environmental design for the multi disciplinary architectural & engineering design studio at Cal Poly, San Luis Obispo and also leads the Green Building Design Course at UCLA for the Ziman Center for Real Estate, a joint center between the UCLA Anderson School of Management and the UCLA School of Law. His current portfolio of work includes both the iconic intermodal transportation stations in San Francisco and Anaheim that will form part of the future California high speed rail link. Recent sustainable masterplan work has included Shanghai Airport City and Beijing Central Business District Design Competitions.

Jesse Reiser, Nanako Umemoto - Reiser + Umemoto

Jesse Reiser received his Bachelor of Architecture degree from the Cooper Union in New York and completed his Masters of Architecture at the Cranbrook Academy of Art. He was a fellow of the American Academy in Rome in 1985 and he worked for the offices of John Hejduk and Aldo Rossi prior to forming Reiser + Umemoto with partner, Nanako Umemoto. Jesse is an Associate Professor of Architecture at Princeton University and has previously taught at various schools in the US and Asia, including Columbia University, Yale University, Ohio State University, Hong Kong University.

Nanako Umemoto received her Bachelor of Architecture from Cooper Union in New York in 1983, following studies at the School of Urban Design and Landscape Architecture at the Osaka University of Art, and formed Reiser + Umemoto with partner, Jesse Reiser in 1986. Nanako Ayelet Karmon currently teaches at the University of Pennsylvania, and has previously taught at various schools in the US and Asia, including Harvard University, Columbia University, Hong Kong University, Kyoto University, Pratt Institute, and the Cooper Union.

Reiser + Umemoto, RUR Architecture, PC, an internationally recognized multidisciplinary design firm, which has built projects at a wide range of scales: from furniture design, to residential and commercial structures, up to the scale of landscape, urban design, and infrastructure. Reiser + Umemoto published the Atlas of Novel Tectonics, in 2006, and recently released the Japanese edition in 2008. They have recently won the Taipei Pop Music Center Competition, scheduled to begin construction in 2012, and their office tower O-14 is currently under construction in Dubai, and is scheduled to be completed in late 2010. The work of Reiser + Umemoto has been published and exhibited widely, and the firm was awarded the Chrysler Award for Excellence in Design in 1999. Jesse Reiser and Nanako Umemoto received the Academy Award in Architecture by the American Academy of Arts and Letters in 2000, and in May of 2008, the Presidential Citation from President George Campbell of the Cooper Union for outstanding practical and theoretical contributions to the field of Architecture.

Winka Dubbeldam, Archi-Tectonics

Winka Dubbeldam is the principal of Archi-Tectonics NY, founded in 1994 and Archi-Tectonics NL, founded in 1997. Dubbeldam is a graduate of the Academy of Architecture in Rotterdam [1990], and received a Degree in Master of Science in Advanced Architectural Design from Columbia University, NYC in 1992. She has lectured extensively and taught at the Masters Programs of Columbia University, NYC, and Harvard University, Cambridge and currently holds the position of Director of the PP@PD, the Post-Professional Program at the University of Pennsylvania, Philadelphia. She has also served as juror in design competitions among which the AIA and the Architecture League, NY, as well as in a multiplicity of reviews at International Architecture Schools. Winka is also an external examiner for the RIBA/ARB at the Architectural Association, London, and serves on the Board of Directors of the Institute for Urban Design, NYC.

Morphosis Architects

Founded in 1972, Morphosis is an interdisciplinary practice involved in rigorous design and research that yields innovative, iconic buildings and urban environments. With founder Thom Mayne serving as design director, the firm today consists of a group of more than 50 professionals, who remain committed to the practice of architecture as a collaborative enterprise. With projects worldwide, the firm's work ranges in scale from residential, institutional, and civic buildings to large urban planning projects. Named after the Greek term, morphosis, meaning to form or be in formation, Morphosis is a dynamic and evolving practice that responds to the shifting and advancing social, cultural, political, and technological conditions of modern life. Over the past 30 years, Morphosis has received 25 Progressive Architecture awards, over 90 American Institute of Architects (AIA) awards, and numerous other honors.

Peer-Reviewed Projects (in order of Appearance)

Ayelet Karmon, Mette Ramsgard Thomsen, Eyal Shaeffer

Ayelet Karmon is an architect, lecturer, and faculty member of the Department of Interior – Building and Environment Design at Shenkar College of Engineering and Design. Her academic role in the department includes the coordination of the design studio studies in addition to the final-year design studio, where she acts as a studio instructor. Ms. Karmon is the initiator of a number of collaborations between her Department, the Textile Design Laboratory, and the Plastics Center at Shenkar, as well as industrial collaborations outside of academia in areas such as material exploration, fabrication processes, and technological innovation in design. These collaborations led to the initiation of the Architectural Knitted Workshop Series, workshops that invited participants to explore the potential of three-dimensional knitted surfaces as models for thinking about the architectural environment. Ms. Karmon has a B.Arch with honors from the Technion, Israel Institute of Technology, and a M.Arch from the Graduate School of Design, Harvard University. Lately, her academic research focuses on the implications of physical and imbedded computing on the design process and interaction with the built environment. She is a partner in Strata Architects, an architectural practice situated in Tel-Aviv.

Mette Ramsgard Thomsen is an architect working with digital technologies. Through a focus on intelligent programming and ideas of emergence, she explores how computational logics can lead to new spatial concepts. Mette's work is practice lead and through projects such as Slow Furl, Strange Metabolisms, Vivisection and Sea Unsea, she investigates the relationship between computational design, craft, and technology. Her research focuses on the Digital Crafting as way of thinking about material practice, computation, and fabrication as part of architectural culture. Mette Ramsgard Thomsen is Associate Professor at the Royal Academy of Fine Arts, School of Architecture, where she heads the Centre for Information Technology and Architecture [CITA]. During the last 5 years, Mette has successfully built the centre that now includes 14 active researchers and research students.

Rodolphe el-Khoury, Nashid Nabian

Rodolphe el-Khoury is Canada Research Chair in Architecture and Urban Design and principal at Khoury Levit Fong. He is the author of numerous critically acclaimed books in architectural history and theory and a regular contributor to professional and academic journals. His books include, Monolithic Architecture, Architecture: in Fashion, Shaping the City; Studies in History, Theory and Urban Design, and See Through Ledoux, Architecture, Theatre, and the Pursuit of Transparency. He has received several awards and international recognition for his design work as principal at Office dA, ReK Productions and, currently, at KLF. el-Khoury is particularly interested in architectural applications for advanced information technology aiming for enhanced responsiveness and sustainability in the build environment.

Nashid Nabian has a doctoral degree in design from Harvard Graduate School of Design where she completed her dissertation on digitally augmented spaces, responsive environment and interactive architectures. She also holds graduate degrees in architecture (Iran) and urban design (University of Toronto). Her interest in spatial practices is focused on the conception of inhabitable spaces that are capable of accommodating a multiplicity of states and are in constant flux in response to needs and desires of their inhabitants. This approach towards design is manifested both in the projects of Arsh Studio—a design office based in Tehran where she is a partner and principal of four—and in her collaborative, interactive art installations.

Future City Labs - Jason Kelly Johnson, Nataly Gattegno

Future Cities Lab is an experimental design and research office based in San Francisco, CA. Design principals Jason Kelly Johnson and Nataly Gattegno have collaborated on a range of award-winning projects exploring the intersections of architecture with advanced fabrication technologies, responsive building systems, and urban space. Their work has been published and exhibited worldwide. Most recently, they were the 2008-09 Muschenheim and Oberdick Fellows at the University of Michigan TCAUP, the 2009 New York Prize Fellows at the Van Alen Institute in New York City, and exhibited work at the 2009-10 Hong Kong / Shenzhen Biennale. Both Johnson and Gattegno studied at Princeton University. They currently teach at CCA and UC Berkeley, as well as workshops including the Architectural Association Visiting School "Biodynamic Structures" and "Hydra-Cities Lab" in Athens, Greece. Jason has also recently collaborated with Andy Payne on the Firefly for Grasshopper toolbar and Primer. Most recently Future Cities Lab has been published in Subnature: Architecture's Other Environments by David Gissen (Princeton Architectural Press, 2009), the "Territory" issue of the AD Journal (2010), and Softspace: From a Representation of Form to a Simulation of Space (Edited by Lally and Young, 2009). The Xeromax Sensing Envelope was produced for the Envelopes show organized by Christopher Hight at the Pratt Manhattan Gallery in January 2010.

Mahesh Senagala,

Joshua Vermillion, Elizabeth Boone, Eric Brockmeyer, Adam Buente, and Kyle Perry are recent graduates of Ball State University's professional Master of Architecture program, former Graduate Student Fellows at the Institute for Digital Fabrication, and founders of PROJECTiONE—a knowledge/research organization and commercial enterprise focused on the relationships between digital and analog processes in design and fabrication (http://projectione.com).

MorphoLuminescence was one of several student projects undertaken for "An Inconvenient Studio," an innovative design course at Ball State leveraging applied research to create new design knowledge focusing on active and responsive systems and environments. "An Inconvenient Studio" was taught by Mahesh Senagala and Joshua Vermillion.

Mahesh Senagala is the Chairman, Professor and Emerging Media fellow at Ball State University's Department of Architecture. Senagala is a past president of the Association for Computer Aided Design in Architecture (ACADIA), an advisory board member of International Digital Media and Arts Association (iDMAa), and an editorial board member of International Journal of Architectural Computing (IJAC). Joshua Vermillion is a faculty member at Ball State University's Department of Architecture, where he helps manage the Institute for Digital Fabrication.

Arshia Mahmoodi, Reza Bagerzadeh

Arshia has received his Masters degree in Architecture and Urban Design from the University of Shahid Beheshti in Tehran in 1997. He further expanded his studies in film television and new media at UCLA in Los Angeles. In Iran, he worked with Bahram Shirdel and Jeffrey Kipnis as the project Architect for the Tehran International Airport among several other experiences. In the United States, he was the principal architect at the studio of Michele Saee for two years winning two major competitions for the firm aside from several other projects that he designed and realized. In 2003, Arshia launched null.lab with his partner Reza Bagherzadeh, an architectural design, research, and implementation firm.

Arshia's work has been published in the United States, Iran, Italy, Dubai, UK and Japan. His design for the Bobco Metals Company garnered much attention from the media after receiving and AIA award.

While in Iran, he was the recipient of several design awards including the 10th annual Japan Architect membrane design competition. He has also been interviewed by several publications, has lectured California Polytechnic State University and been a guest critic at SCI_Arc , CalPoly Pomona, University of Southern California, Woodbury University and Los Angeles Institute of Architecture and Design. Arshia is currently the principal of Void, inc. and in collaboration with partner Axel Schmitzberger, they operate as '11.1' where the practice is dedicated to the exploration of 'extreme' conditions in various notions of space.

Reza Bagherzadeh gleans inspiration from studying abstract lines in nature, art, technology, and graffiti. He moved to the Midwest from Tehran at the age of 9 before his family settled in Los Angeles where he attended high school. As a teenager he was drawn in by the hip hop and graffiti culture which conversely influenced his decision to become an architect. Reza enrolled in the esteemed Southern California Institute for Architecture (SCI-Arc) and immediately resonated with the process. While in school, he landed positions working for architects Bahram Shirdel and Jeffrey Kipnis and went on to win numerous international competitions.

Upon graduation, he and his partners launched their own design and build firm, Back Studios, which they ran for the next two years. In 1994, Reza partnered in a stone fabrication shop that he still owns and operates today. Over the next eight years, Reza held positions with world renown architects including Frank Gehry, Michele Saee, and Eric Owen Moss. In 1996, he returned to Bahram Shirdel's firm and spent a year in his native Iran where he worked as the designer on both the International Airport and the Museum of Water. During that auspicious time, he met Arshia with whom he would later form null.lab.

Urbana, Rob Ley

Rob Ley is the founding principal of Urbana, an architecture and design studio based in Los Angeles. Urbana engages current material and formal technologies to develop environments that respond to human inhabitation and experience. The studio's recent experimental work includes installations at the Storefront for Art and Architecture, and the Taubman Museum of Art. The studio was recently awarded the Upjohn grant from the AIA, a Graham Foundation grant, and an IDEC grant in support of current research with shape changing material applications in architecture.

Mr. Ley currently teaches graduate and undergraduate design studios and seminars at the Southern California Institute of Architecture (SCI-Arc). He holds a Master of Architecture from the University of California, Los Angeles (2000) and a Bachelor of Science in Architecture from the University of Illinois, Urbana-Champaign (1996).

Prior to founding Urbana, Rob was a project manager at Randall Stout Architects (Los Angeles), DMAC Architecture (Chicago), and senior designer at Cliff Garten Studio (Los Angeles)

Jonas Coersmeier

Jonas Coersmeier is an award-winning architect whose work has been published internationally. Jonas worked as a management consultant for McKinsey & Co. before co-founding his first design practice, Probehead LLC, in 2001, with specialization in 3D online environments. Currently, he is a partner of the architectural design firm Büro NY, with offices in New York and Berlin.

Jonas also teaches design studios and research seminars at The Pratt Institute, where he leads the international design studio 'Pratt Berlin.' Previously, he has taught at the University of Pennsylvania, and directed the Digital Design Department at the University of Kassel, Germany.

His work explores the relationships between science and culture through computational design techniques. In particular, his projects pair nanotechnology with algorithmic tools to study natural systems. For instance, studies of the nano-scale patterns of silk led to the New Silk Road project (2006), research into engineered and natural "green" produced the Queen's Plaza project (2001), and explorations of the operative concepts of cell formation guided both his RWTH Aachen project (2009) and his entry for the WTC Memorial design competition (2003). His WTC Memorial design was shortlisted as a finalist and first runner-up. Jonas' work has previously been published by ACADIA in 1996 as part of Bill Mitchell's "Studio of the Future" at MIT. Jonas received his Masters Degree from Columbia University (w/ honors) and his Engineering diplom from TU-Darmstadt.

architectuREdefined - Joseph Choma

architectuREdefined; Joseph Choma is a computation based researcher focused on new emerging architectural consequences, by means of morphological design machines. Joseph graduated with a Bachelor of Architecture from Rensselaer Polytechnic Institute and currently attends postgraduate studies in Design and Computation at Massachusetts Institute of Technology. He presently teaches an advanced workshop titled trans-FORM: Embodying Instrumentality / Embracing Uncertainty as an Adjunct Professor at the Boston Architectural College.

He has been recognized in ten design competitions at both the academic, local, and international levels. His designs have been published in magazines such as Design Exchange, eVolo, and Plan amongst others. His work has been exhibited in China, Columbia, England, India, Italy, and in the United States (MA, NV, NY, PA). He has previously worked for Acconci Studio, Carlos Zapata Studio, and Gage Clemenceau Architects. Joseph was also the Curator and Designer for Grimshaw's EMPAC Architecture and Design Exhibition in New York. He also developed the geometry of peripersonal space for Ted Krueger's sensory research.

Joseph's most recent research focuses on theoretical ideas associated with instrumentality and artificial intelligence. He is currently developing a designer's guide into point set topology, which explores combing tacit and explicit learning within the realm of mathematics.

Ming Tang, Jonathon R. Anderson

Ming Tang is an assistant professor at the University of Cincinnati. He is also the founder of Tang & Yang Architects. He earned his Master of Architecture degree in Tsinghua University, China in 2000. His research includes parametric design, BIM, GIS, virtual reality, simulation and fabrication.

Jonathon R. Anderson is currently an assistant professor of Interior Architecture at the University of North Carolina Greensboro. He received his Masters of Fine Arts (MFA) from Savannah College of Art & Design in 2009 and a bachelor in architecture from Southern Illinois University in 2007. Jonathon's research explores the progression of design in the digital realm through algorithmic, generative, and scripted parameters. His research utilizes digital fabrication technologies to realize dynamic computer models in the static physical world.

Bob Trempe

Bob Trempe's work focuses on new methods of information visualization and how emergent information can serve as instruction for architectural production. Thought of as the study of process itself, Bob's works are typically articulated through procedural techniques and the deployment of repetitious systems, exploiting time-based qualities to notate, visualize, and analyze changes-in-state. Time plays a critical role in his explorations of natural, man-made, and intangible phenomena as time is the living, breathing dimension of architecture. Toolsets and methodologies of practice found in applications such as Grasshopper, Houdini, and Rhinoceros are exploited based on the relationships of tool to task. Outputs via planar fabrication, vector-based narrations, and composite imagery are employed as part of the experimentation of process-in-pipeline.

Examples of his research can be seen through his office Dis-section Architectural and Media Design (DAMD) www.dis-section.com. Speculative projects such as "Slpistream" can be seen in the 2006 Birkhauser book "Distinguishing Digital Architecture." Investigate constructions have been shown nationally and internationally at venues such as the 2007 and 2009 ACM/SIGGRAPH Art Galleries as well as exhibits such as DrawingOut2010 in Melbourne, Australia.

Bob Trempe is currently an Assistant Professor of Architecture at Temple University in Philadelphia PA.

Easton+Combs - Lonn Combs, Rona Easton

Lonn Combs studied architecture at the University of Kentucky, where he received his first professional degree in architecture in 1992. He received a post-professional degree at Columbia University, in 2001.

Lonn Combs co-founded Easton+Combs in 2004 with over ten years of professional experience in Germany, China, and the U.S. He received professional licensure in Germany in 1996 and in the U.S. in 2002. In tandem with the founding of Easton+Combs, he has taught design studios at Pratt Institute, City College of New York, and Cornell University. He has served as the Assistant Chair and the Acting Chair of the Department of Undergraduate Architecture at Pratt Institute from 2007 to 2010.

Rona Easton studied architecture at the University of Strathclyde in Glasgow, Scotland and completed her Diploma in Architecture at the University of Westminster in London, England in 1990. She holds a Masters degree in the history and theory of architecture from the Bartlett School of Architecture in London which she received in 1988. She has been a registered architect in the United Kingdom since 1991 and in the United States since 2003 (in the state of New York). She is also a LEED Accredited Professional and is focused on sustainable research, planning, and design.

Rona Easton worked professionally in the U.K., Germany, China, and the United States before co-founding Easton+Combs. Since her arrival in New York City in 1998, she has been the managing architect and overseen the completion of several projects in the New York metropolitan area totaling over half a million square feet of built area.

ARUP & Architectural Association—Maria Mingallon, Sakthivel Ramaswamy, Konstantinos Karatzas

Maria Mingallon [Msc MEng CEng MICE] is a chartered structural engineer with a degree in architecture. She studied at UCLM and Imperial College (one year scholarship), graduating in 2005. She has worked at Arup since then as a Structural Engineer. Among other projects, she has designed two footbridges leading to the London 2012 Olympic Park. In 2008, Arup sponsored her Msc in Emergent Technologies and Design at the Architectural Association for which she was awarded Distinction. She has taught at the Architectural Association as a visiting tutor and she is currently Adjunct Professor at McGill School of Architecture in Montreal.

Sakthivel Ramaswamy [B.Des. M.Arch] is an architect and researcher involved in transient and adaptive environmental smart systems. He explores advanced fabrication techniques and generative design processes. He is a recipient of Smt. Kamlaben Gambhirchand Award for excellence in research for his published work 'Biomimicry- an Analysis of Contemporary Biomimetic Approaches' in 2007. He was awarded M.Arch in Emergent Technologies and Design from the Architectural Association in 2010, and B.Des [Hons.] from CEPT University, Ahmedabad in 2006.

Konstantinos Karatzas [MEng MSc MBA] is an entrepreneur and researcher with a background in engineering, and interest in smart materials, biomimetics, lightweight structures, and advanced simulation and analysis techniques. He was awarded an MBA from Imperial College Business School, an MSc with Distinction in Emergent Technologies + Design from the Architectural Association in 2009, and his MEng in Civil Engineering from the Polytechnic School of of Thessaloniki in 2008.

Brennan Buck, David Freeland, David Fletcher

Brennan Buck is principal of FreelandBuck in New York and a Critic at the Yale School of Architecture. From 2004–2008, he was assistant professor at the University of Applied Arts, Vienna teaching in Studio Greg Lynn. He has practiced both landscape architecture and architecture, having worked for Neil M. Denari Architects and Johnston Marklee & Associates in Los Angeles. He is a graduate of Cornell University and the UCLA Department of Architecture and Urban Design.

David Freeland is principal of FreelandBuck in Los Angeles and adjunct faculty at Woodbury University. With over 10 years of experience in architecture, he has worked on award winning projects with a number offices in New York and Los Angeles including Michael Maltzan Architecture, Roger Sherman Architecture and Urban Design, RES4, AGPS, and Eisenman Architects. He is a graduate of University of Virginia and the UCLA Department of Architecture and Urban Design.

David Fletcher is the founder and managing principal of Fletcher Studio Landscape Architecture + Urban Design. His work, which includes large-scale planning projects, institutions, public spaces, commercial and multi-family residential development, is known for its innovative approaches to landscape architecture in the built environment. Fletcher Studio's proposal for a comprehensive and sustainable master plan for Downtown Dallas placed 1st in the international design competition, Revision Dallas. Additionally, the firm recently placed 2nd in an international design and planning competition, "A New Infrastructure," sponsored by sci_Arc and the Architect's Newspaper. His work is currently on exhibit at the University of Toronto, UC Berkeley, The MAK Center, and sci_Arc.

Populous & Buro Happold, Alan R Tansey, Michael Westlake, Joe White, Ian Keough

Alan R Tansey was born in a rural part of Ohio between the heights of the Appalachians and the plains of the Midwest. Alan studied at Kent State University as an undergraduate and participated in the College of Architecture's international studies program in Florence, Italy. Continuing his education in New York, he fulfilled his Master's degree at Columbia University's GSAPP program where he also discovered architectural photography. The mix of technical education, international study, conceptual design, and photography have influenced much of Alan's work today. He is currently a designer at Populous working on world renowned futbol and athletic stadia. In parallel with his design work, Alan spends much of his free time documenting architecture, interiors, installations, and bicycles in the photographic medium. His photographic work has been published in international magazines, journals, and numerous web publications.

Michael Westlake was born in the south-east of England, U.K. and is an associate in Populous's International Design Studio in New York. After finishing Art College he studied Architecture at the Welsh School of Architecture in Cardiff, Wales and at the South Bank University, London, England. He is project architect on Club de Futbol, Monterrey, Mexico, an AIA award winning 50,000-seat soccer stadium, and Estadio das Dunas in Natal, Brazil, for the 2014 World Cup. For the past three years he has been a team leader in the New York Studio, involved in the design direction of many of Populous's major international projects. Michael is also involved in the research and development of parametric software tools to enhance stadium bowl generation and design. He is an advisor on the MLS (Major League Soccer) stadium design guide.

Joe White, P.E. received his Masters in Civil and Architectural Engineering from the University of Bath, England, and is currently a Senior Structural Engineer with Buro Happold's New York office. In addition to his work on the Monterrey Stadium, Joe has worked on a number of high profile global sports projects including: Emirates Stadium in London, Arena das Dunas in Brazil, Sochi 2014 Olympic Stadium in Russia, Brian Lara Cricket Academy in Trinidad, and the Turin 2006 Olympic Speed Skating Arena in Italy. Joe also has experience outside of the sports sector; notable projects include the Isabella Stewart Gardner Museum in Boston, the King Abdullah Financial District in Saudi Arabia, and Harvard University's Allston Science Complex in Boston. He has been a visiting lecturer at Columbia University Graduate School of Architecture, Planning and Preservation and is currently Adjunct Professor of Engineering at the New York Institute of Technology.

Ian Keough received his Bachelor of Fine Arts in Sculpture from the University of Michigan and his Masters of Architecture from Parsons The New School for Design. Ian has worked for Buro Happold's New York office since 2005, and is currently an Associate with the Technical Engineering group. Ian's vast knowledge of the fabrication industry has made him fundamental to the integration of Building Information Modeling technologies throughout Buro Happold world-wide. Through scripting and programming, he has developed tools for the linking of various modeling and analytical programs. Ian has also taken a lead role in the modeling and documentation of specific projects, most notably for Monterrey Stadium in Mexico, Arena das Dunas in Brazil, Brian Lara Cricket Academy in Trinidad, World Trade Center Memorial Pavillion in New York, Phoenix Civic Space Sculpture in Phoenix, Arizona, United States Institute of Peace in Washington, D.C., and the Crystal Bridges Museum of American Art in Bentonville, Arkansas. Ian also founded the company goBim in 2008 through which he has developed building model viewing applications for smart phones and tablet devices.

SPAN, Matias del Campo, Sandra Manninger

Matias del Campo studied architecture at the University of Applied Arts Vienna, Austria, participated in a 2006 research visit in Los Angeles in the United States. He was awarded a Schindler Scholarship, for the MAK Artists and Architects-in-Residence Program, a guest professorship at the Dessau Institute of Architecture, and the ESARQ, Universidad Internacional de Catalunya, and curated the Architectural Biennale in Beijing, 2008, 2010 South American Section.

Sandra Manninger studied architecture at the Vienna University of Technology in Austria, participated in a 2006 Research visit in Los Angeles in the United States, awarded a Schindler Scholarship, for the MAK Artists and Architects-in-Residence Program, was a guest lecturer at the Dessau Institute of Architecture and guest professor at the ESARQ, Universidad Internacional de Catalunya.

SPANs obsessive explorations of contemporary moods (Lavin, S.) are fueled by the opulent repertoire of formations in nature as well as form as a driving force at large. The underlying presence of curvilinear desires reflects back and radiates in conditions informed by a manifold of cultural lineages such as Baroque geometries or the presence of the endless in Frederick Kieslers work. The latent abilities dormant in creative strategies driven by algorithmic and generative processes, the simulation of environmental pressures, the desire to speculate about architectural opportunities in the presence of animated matter generate opulent, intensive spatial conditions reflecting the cravings of SPAN for contemporary atmospheres.

Credits

ACADIA Elected Officers President: **Nancy Cheng** *pres@acadia.org* ACADIA Appointed Officers Secretary, **Aron Temkin**, *secretary@acadia.org* Treasurer, **Marc Swackhamer**, *treasurer@acadia.org* Membership, **Anijo Mathew**, *membership@acadia.org* Awards Committee **Omar Khan**, *chair awards@acadia.org* **Karen Kensek**, Aron Temkin Elections Committee **Mike Christenson**, *Chair elections@acadia.org* **Wassim Jabi, Michael Fox** Webmaster, **Mike Christenson**, *webmaster@acadia.org* Web Communications, **Andrew Kudless**, **Anijo Mathew**, and **Mike Christenson** Print Publications, Greg Luhan 2010 Conference Team, LIFE:in:formation *acadia2010@acadia.org* Conference chairs: **Aaron Sprecher**, Assistant Professor, McGill University **Shai Yeshayahu**, Associate Professor, Southern Illinois University **Pablo Lorenzo-Eiroa**, Associate Professor Adjunct, The Cooper Union Exhibition Chairs: **Chandler Ahrens**, Architect Partner, Open Source Architecture **Axel Schmitzberger**, Associate Professor, California State Polytechnic University, Pomona **Michael Wen-Sen Su**, Visiting Assistant Professor, Pratt Institute Webmaster: **Axel Schmitzberger** Steering Committee 2008 (Oct 2008 - Oct 2010) **Larry Barrow**, Mississippi State University, *lbarrow@caad.msstate.edu* **Philip Beesley**, Waterloo, *pbeesley@uwaterloo.ca* **Wassim Jabi**, Cardiff University, Wales, *wassim.jabi@gmail.com* **Andrew Kudless**, California College of the Arts, *andrew@materialsystems.org* **Marc Swackhamer**, University of Minnesota, *swack004@umn.edu* Alternates:**Omar Khan**, SUNY Buffalo, *omarkhan@buffalo.edu* **Anijo Mathew**, IIT Chicago Institute of Design, *anijo@id.iit.edu* **Mo Zell**, University of Wisconsin, Milwaukee, *zell@uwm.edu* 2009 (Oct 2009 - Oct 2011) **Mike Christenson**, North Dakota State University, *michael.a.christenson@gmail.com* **Gregory Luhan**, University of Kentucky, *galuhan@uky.edu* **Anijo Mathew**, IIT Chicago Institute of Design, *anijo@id.iit.edu* **Mahesh Senagala**, Ball State University, **Aron Temkin**, Florida Atlantic University, *atemkin@fau.edu* Alternates: **Karen Kensek**, University of Southern California, *kensek@usc.edu* **Michael Fox**, Cal Poly Pomona, *mafox@foxlin.com* **Mark Cabrinha**, Cal Poly State University, SLO, *mcabrinh@calpoly.edu* 2010 (Oct 2010-Oct 2012) **David Celento Michael Fox** Cal Poly Pomona, *mafox@foxlin.com* **Loukas Kalisperis**, Pennsylvania State University Karen Kensek, University of Southern California, *kensek@usc.edu* **Wei Yan**, Texas A & M Alternate: **Brian Lockyear**

ACADIA 2010 Sponsors

Host Institution:

The Irvin S. Chanin
School of Architecture of
The Cooper Union for the
Advancement of Science and Art
www.cooper.edu

GOLD SPONSOR:

Autodesk

Autodesk® Revit
Autodesk® Ecotect®
www.autodesk.com

BRONZE SPONSOR:

where ideas take shape™
www.solidthinking.com

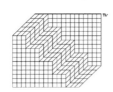

Buro Happold
www.burohappold.com

www.objet.com

www.bentley.com

SPONSORS I:

Rhinoceros®

Rhinoceros Scripting
Rhinoceros Grasshopper
www.mcneel.com
www.rhino3d.com

TischITP

NYU ITP
www.itp.nyu.com

The Pratt Institute, School of Architecture, Thomas Hanrahan, *Dean* Erika Hinrichs, *Acting Chair* Jason Lee, *Acting Assistant Chair* Kurt Everhart, *Assistant to the Dean, Academic Affairs* Chi-Fan Wong, *Director, Siegel Gallery* Latoya Johnson, *Administrative Assistant* Jason Idjadi, *student* Iris Fong, *student* Michael Archer, *student* The School of Architecture of The Cooper Union Host Institution of the ACADIA 2010 Conference Anthony Vidler, *Dean* Elizabeth O'Donnell, *Associate Dean* Monica Shapiro, *Administrative Associate* Pat De Angelis, *Secretary* Emmy Mikelson, *Assistant to the Deans for Public Programs and Research* Steven Hillyer, *Director, Architecture Archive* David Greenstein, *Continuing Education Director* Zulaika Ayub, *Administrative Assistant* ACADIA 2010, *student* Lautaro Cuttica, *student* Ricardo Escutia, *student* Jeremy Jacinth, *student* Henry Mena, *student* Rolando Vega, *student* Danny Wills, *student* Austin Smith, *student* Alan Ruiz, *student* Anna Cero, *Exhibition support student* Jimmy Pan; *student* Jesus Yepez, *student* Fabio Alvino-Roca

The Exhibition Chairs would like to thank ACADIA's Steering committee for providing enormous support and encouragement through the whole process. Our gratitude goes to our respective institutions that have provided us with academic support: McGill University, Southern Illinois University, The Cooper Union.

A special thank to our friends and families who have supported us all along this great journey: Ice Lee, Tony Martínez, Sean @ starfish-prime, Quynh T. Nguyen.

Exhibition Host Institutions:

School of Architecture
at Pratt Institute
www.pratt.edu

The Irvin S. Chanin
School of Architecture of
The Cooper Union for the
Advancement of Science and Art
www.cooper.edu

SPONSORS II:

www.gehrytechnologies.com

Thornton Tomasetti

www.thorntontomasetti.com

rmJm

www.rmjm.com

KPF

KPF architects

www.kpf.com

SOM

SOM architects

www.som.com

Studio Mode

www.studiomode.nu

Z Corporation

www.zcorp.com

ABC Imaging

www.abcimaging.com

Princeton Architectural Press

PAPRESS

www.papress.com

AutoDesSys

www.formz.com

www.mcgill.ca

ActarBirkhäuser Distribution

Actar Publishing

www.actar.com /
www.actar-d.com
www.birkhauser-architecture.com

Vertical Access, TPAS

www.tpasllc.com

ASSOCIATION FOR COMPUTER AIDED DESIGN IN ARCHITECTURE

ACADIA2010

LIFE in:formation

ON RESPONSIVE INFORMATION AND VARIATIONS IN ARCHITECTURE